WHAT DO MORMONS BELIEVE?

WHAT DO MORMONS BELIEVE?

REX E. LEE

Deseret Book Company
Salt Lake City, Utah

For Janet, my inspiration for all good things

Library of Congress Cataloging-in-Publication Data.

Lee, Rex E., 1935–
    What do Mormons believe? / Rex E. Lee.
        p.   cm.
    ISBN 0-87579-639-7
        1. The Church of Jesus Christ of Latter-day Saints — Doctrines.
2. Mormon Church — Doctrines.   I. Title.
BX8635.2.L44   1992
289.3'23 — dc20   92-36087
                                                                          CIP

Printed in the United States of America

10   9   8   7   6

CONTENTS

Contents

CONTENTS

WHY THIS BOOK?

I am a believing, practicing member of The Church of Jesus Christ of Latter-day Saints, commonly known as the Mormon Church, and I write this book about my church. I want to state at the outset what the reader can expect from it and, equally important, what he or she cannot expect from it.

First, it is not an attempt to persuade others to join my church. We are known, frankly, as vigorous proselyters. Missionary work is an essential component of the Church's overall endeavors. I believe in missionary work, and I have participated in it. For two-and-a-half years I devoted my full time to it. This book is not part of that effort. I have written this book not to convert but to explain my church and its beliefs from the point of view of a believer. To be sure, any attempt to explain what one strongly believes will inevitably involve some elements of advocacy, but my purpose here is not so much to persuade as to inform.

Second, the book's informational scope is neither broad nor deep. It is a book that can be read and, I hope, understood in a couple of hours. Persons interested in a more

1

extensive discussion of Mormon doctrine will find that good books are available for that purpose. (See "For Further Reading" at the back of the book.)

Finally, I write because for some time I have felt the need for a relatively succinct and modest statement about my church: what we believe, why we believe, and in light of those beliefs, why we do some of the things we do. It is written principally for the reader who, for whatever reason, would like to understand the Mormon Church, not necessarily for the purpose of joining it, or even defending it, but simply to enlarge his or her understanding the same way one might expand his understanding of another culture, or of history, or of mathematics.

A great irony is that to date the efforts to explain Mormonism in a nonproselyting way have come from persons who do not share the bedrock beliefs on which the religion is based. That observation is not intended as a criticism; I am willing to assume that such efforts were undertaken in good faith. But if I want to gain an understanding of Chinese culture, I can best obtain it from someone who has not only made a thorough study of things Chinese, but, even more importantly, sees the world through Chinese eyes.

If, then, you are interested in learning about Mormonism and why Mormons believe as they do, not necessarily for the purpose of becoming an adherent or a critic, but just so you can be better informed, this book is for you.

CHAPTER 1

THE RESTORATION
OF ALL THINGS:
MODERN-DAY PROPHETS
AND REVELATION

The central message of Mormonism is that there has been a restoration of the church and gospel of Jesus Christ. Now what does that mean? Basically, it means that the church — the organization, its authority, and its ordinances — established by Jesus Christ during his earthly ministry has once again been brought back to earth. It also means that the teachings and revelations of Jesus Christ and his prophets have been taught again fully in modern times. These things were accomplished by our Heavenly Father and his son Jesus Christ, acting through prophets.

Throughout history, whenever God has spoken to his children on earth, he has done so through his prophets. (See 2 Chronicles 29:27; Jeremiah 7:25; Ephesians 4:11; Acts 15:32.) God himself has said he will do nothing save he reveals his words through his servants the prophets. (See Amos 3:7; Ephesians 2:19–20; 1 Corinthians 12:28.) Thus, in these modern times, our Heavenly Father has again spoken through prophets to his children on earth. The things that happened in connection with this modern-day contact between heaven and earth constitute the Restoration, which is the core of Mormonism.

While the atoning sacrifice was the principal purpose for the Savior's earthly mission, it was not the only one. Jesus Christ taught eternal principles that constitute his gospel, and he established his church, the vehicle that would be responsible for preserving and spreading those gospel principles after his death. (See Matthew 16:18; John 15:16.) Some of those gospel principles pertain to the Church itself and its organization. For example, the Apostle Paul taught that the Church was built on a foundation of apostles and prophets. (See 1 Corinthians 12:28; Ephesians 2:20.) Paul also made it quite clear that the fundamental organization was not to change until "all come in the unity of the faith, and of the knowledge of the Son of God, unto a perfect man." (Ephesians 4:13.) This is just another way of saying that as long as humankind exists in its fallible state, the identifying characteristic of Jesus Christ's church will be its organization on the foundation stones of apostles and prophets, Jesus Christ himself being the cornerstone.

For a time, this original church as organized by the Savior endured as established. When one of the twelve apostles died, another was chosen to take his place. (See Acts 1:23–26.) Both the Savior himself and also the ancient apostles prophesied, however, that this was not to last. The Church would be rocked by apostasy (see Matthew 24:5, 9–12, 23–24), and there would be a falling away (see 2 Thessalonians

2:3). Christ's church, the one he established on a foundation of apostles and prophets, would one day not be found upon the earth. What would remain would be churches that had changed in various ways, both doctrinally and organizationally, from the original church.

But those early apostles also spoke of a Restoration, a bringing back of what had been lost, including apostles and prophets. Probably the clearest New Testament prophecy of the Restoration came from Peter in the third chapter of Acts. In verses twenty and twenty-one, Peter said: "He shall send Jesus Christ, which before was preached unto you: whom the heaven must receive until the times of restitution of all things, which God hath spoken by the mouth of all his holy prophets since the world began." (See also Ephesians 1:10.) Our message is that the "restitution of all things," predicted by Peter two thousand years ago, has in fact occurred.

The key figure in the Restoration—the person through whom the Lord worked to bring it about—was the first of the modern prophets, Joseph Smith, Jr.

The first event occurred in the spring of 1820, when Joseph Smith was fourteen. In response to young Joseph's earnest prayer concerning which of the many sects he should join, our Heavenly Father and his Son, Jesus Christ, appeared to him. Part of that visitation included this specific message: He should join none of the churches, because none was true. But Joseph was told that if he remained worthy, God himself would one day restore through him the true teachings, church organization, and priesthood authority of Jesus Christ.

Following that initial vision in 1820, the Prophet Joseph

Smith had a series of other visits from heavenly messengers, each with a specific purpose and message. The three most important of the experiences are these:

(1) Joseph Smith received a series of annual visits from an angel named Moroni. Fourteen hundred years earlier, Moroni had been the last custodian of the records of a people who had inhabited the American continents. The records, which Moroni and his predecessors had kept on metal plates, were religious in nature, like the Bible, consisting mainly of revelations from God to his prophets. They also contained, however, historical data and descriptions of how the people lived and how they governed themselves.

As a resurrected being, Moroni appeared to Joseph Smith and showed him the site of a set of records on gold plates that Joseph would one day translate. At least once a year from 1823 to 1827, Moroni met Joseph Smith at the site, and in his final visit, the angel delivered the set of plates to him. The records that Moroni delivered were principally a compilation prepared by his father from all their people's records. His father's name was Mormon, and the set of metal plates that Moroni gave to Joseph Smith and that Joseph later translated by the inspiration of God bore the title the Book of Mormon, because Mormon was the principle compiler.

(2) During the course of translating the Book of Mormon, Joseph Smith and his scribe, Oliver Cowdery, learned of the importance of baptism. The Book of Mormon (as does the New Testament) frequently mentions baptism as an ordinance involving water, necessary for membership in the Lord's church and for forgiveness of sins. Near the Susquehanna River, on May 15, 1829, the two inquired of the Lord

concerning baptism. In response, they were visited by John the Baptist, the New Testament prophet. He laid his hands on their heads and conferred upon them the Aaronic Priesthood, which carries with it the authority to baptize. Following this ordination, and acting pursuant to John the Baptist's instructions, Joseph and Oliver baptized one other, wading into the river and entirely immersing each other in the water.

The Aaronic Priesthood was the authority by which Aaron and his sons and the tribe of Levi administered the law of Moses, as described in the Old Testament. This priesthood, however, did not have the authority to perform the full range of priesthood ordinances or fully govern the church established by Jesus Christ. In that sense, it was, and is, a "lesser" priesthood.

(3) Shortly after the visit of John the Baptist, a priesthood of greater authority, the Melchizedek Priesthood, was restored to Joseph Smith and Oliver Cowdery by the three presiding New Testament apostles, Peter, James, and John. This priesthood contains the authority of the apostleship; thus Joseph Smith and Oliver Cowdery became the first modern-day apostles. The Melchizedek Priesthood bears the power to do what the Lord described to Peter: "Whatsoever ye shall bind on earth shall be bound in heaven: and whatsoever ye shall loose on earth shall be loosed in heaven." (Matthew 18:18.) The restoration of these two priesthoods brought to the earth once again the power to act in the name of, and on behalf of, the Savior himself.

With this authority, and after a commandment to do so by the Lord, on April 6, 1830, Joseph Smith and Oliver Cowdery organized The Church of Jesus Christ of Latter-day

Saints (nicknamed the Mormon Church). The Church grew rapidly, and the foundation of apostles and prophets was laid within the first few years. That foundation is still intact today—the Church is led by a council of twelve apostles and a presidency of three presiding prophets (much like Peter, James, and John).

The response of many people to the sequence of direct contacts between heaven and earth—involving no lesser figures than the Father and the Son; an ancient, hitherto unheard-of New World prophet; John the Baptist; and Peter, James, and John—is likely to be one of incredulity. How could anyone possibly believe that things like that could happen in modern times? To this response, I make two comments.

First, I not only believe, but know that it happened. No, I was not there in 1820 when Joseph Smith saw the Father and the Son. Neither was it my privilege to be present at the Susquehanna River in 1829 when first John the Baptist and later Peter, James, and John appeared to Joseph Smith and Oliver Cowdery. Instead, I know through the power of the Holy Ghost, which the Lord has promised will teach the truth to his disciples and testify of him (see John 14:16–17, 26; 15:26; 16:7–14), so that not seeing, they may believe (see John 20:29). This testimony is available to all who enquire of God with honesty, desire, and faith. (See James 1:5–6.)

Second, these contemporary revelations are no more unusual than the accounts of angelic visitations contained in both the Old and New Testaments. If you accept those as true, then does not the possibility of modern-day revelation follow as a matter of course? The scriptures assure us that God is "the same yesterday, and to day, and for ever" (Hebrews 13:8; see also Psalms 102:27; Malachi 3:6); that he "will do nothing, [save] he revealeth his secret unto his servants the prophets" (Amos 3:7); and that apostles and prophets are necessary until all come to a unity of the faith (see Ephesians 4:11–13).

Is there any reason to assume any lesser need in today's world for prophets and direct revelation than in millennia already past? Indeed, can there be any serious doubt that if comparisons were to be made, the need today for direct guidance is greater than it has ever been in the past? Do you believe that God gave Moses guidance for the people of his day? Or that Jehovah spoke to his people through Isaiah, Jeremiah, and other prophets? Can you really give me any good reason why things should be different in today's world? Do you really think our need for heavenly guidance has disappeared? Or that God does not care about such things today, or is past caring for his modern-day children?

Certainly the Bible has openly prophesied of God's active involvement in our world. There are the numerous prophecies in Isaiah and Ezekiel and other prophetic books about the gathering of Israel, which is part of the Restoration, the ongoing "restitution of all things." There is John's vision of the great battles of the Lamb of God against the forces of evil, of prophets and miracles. Are these kinds of things never to come? Or is it a matter of disbelieving what the prophets have promised?

Claims of angelic visitations and divine revelation are not outrageous unless one regards the Bible itself as outrageous. And think of the consequences if it really is true.

It means that once again, in these modern times, our Heavenly Father has reestablished contact between the heavens and the earth. It means that we need not guess concerning his will for his people. It means that Jesus Christ, in whom we believe, is no mythic figure but truly is the living God and Savior of this world.

CHAPTER 2

THE BOOK OF MORMON: ANOTHER TESTAMENT OF JESUS CHRIST

Overstating the importance of the Book of Mormon to The Church of Jesus Christ of Latter-day Saints would be difficult. The most modest statement that could be made about the Book of Mormon is that it is one of four books recognized by Church members as scripture. The other three are the King James Bible (consisting of both the Old and New Testaments), the Doctrine and Covenants (a collection of 138 revelations given to Joseph Smith and later prophets), and the Pearl of Great Price (a short compilation of translation, revelation, and Church history and belief).

Beyond this, the Book of Mormon, more than any other scripture or individual, has provided the vehicle through which Church members have gained a personal conviction that the Restoration really has occurred. It has also been the Church's most effective missionary tool.

Largely because of the extraordinary circumstances under which it came into existence, the Book of Mormon has

11

been subject to intense and long-standing scrutiny by scholars and critics. Very simply, it has withstood the test of time. Efforts to disprove it have been unavailing. The book was produced in a period of about three months by a twenty-two-year-old man with little formal training or education. Yet it is a complex work of more than five hundred pages, similar to the historical, doctrinal, and revelatory nature of the Old or New Testament, divided into numerous books claiming different authorship. Only one decent explanation exists as to how the book came about and how it has survived 160 years of the most searching examination. That explanation is the one given by the man who brought it into existence: Under divine instruction and power, Joseph Smith translated it from a set of records given to him by a heavenly messenger.

To be sure, there are several objective indicators that Joseph Smith's account of the book's origin is true. Some of the evidences are based on archaeological findings, and some, on the book's structure and word patterns. They are consistent with the conclusion that the Book of Mormon could not have been written by a single author living in the early nineteenth century. (For references on such evidences, see "For Further Reading" at the back of the book.)

I find such evidences interesting but not critical. All such studies are, by their very nature, inconclusive. More important, however, is the fact that such evidences do not and cannot provide the real basis for understanding the truthfulness of the Book of Mormon. The primary evidence lies elsewhere. The book itself discloses the only way by which such an understanding can be obtained. In the very last chapter of the book, verse four, Moroni gave the following promise to all who would read the record: "When ye shall receive these things, I would exhort you that ye would ask God, the Eternal Father, in the name of Christ, if these things are not true; and if ye shall ask with a sincere heart, with real intent, having faith in Christ, he will manifest the truth of it unto you, by the power of the Holy Ghost."

The most important reason for the prominent role the Book of Mormon plays in the lives of individual Church members is tied to Moroni's promise. For Mormons, there is no more frequently cited scripture. And with good reason. The Book of Mormon, both in its origin and in its content, is inextricably linked to the Restoration. If Joseph Smith really saw and did the things that he said he saw and did, then the Book of Mormon has to be true. And it also follows, if the Book of Mormon is true, then Joseph Smith's claims are accurate and truthful.

Accordingly, Moroni's great promise — if, after reading the record with a sincere heart, you ask Heavenly Father whether the things written in the Book of Mormon are true, God himself will reveal its truth to you — provides a simple, though profound, key to testing the message of the Restoration. I think I can safely say that all Mormons who really understand their religion, and for whom that religion plays an important part in their lives, have undergone the process of which Moroni spoke. In one way or another, they have sought and received the assurance that Moroni promised. That is the basic reason why the Book of Mormon is so important to us. The authenticity of Mormonism stands or falls with the book from which the Church derives its nickname.

What, then, is this book? It is the story of three groups of people who inhabited the American continent hundreds of years ago. All three groups came from the Mideast. One left at the time the Tower of Babel was built, and the other two about 600 B.C., during the days of the prophet Jeremiah, one group shortly before and the other during the fall of Jerusalem. As was the case in the Old World, these New World peoples had among them prophets whose words, because they came from God, were scripture.

The record concerning the earliest group is quite short. It consists of 1 book out of 15—or 32 pages out of 522. These people were called the Jaredites, and the book devoted to them is called the Book of Ether. The Jaredites grew to a multimillion-membered society that existed from the time of the Tower of Babel to about 400–500 B.C. They lasted until about two hundred years after the later groups arrived, though the contact between the Jaredites and the later groups was limited to a single survivor of the last great Jaredite battle. (See Omni 1:21—most of the scripture-like references not in the Bible, such as 1 Nephi 3:7 or Alma 34:13, are to the Book of Mormon. Citations to the Doctrine and Covenants are designated simply as "D&C," while citations to "Abraham," "Moses," or "Joseph Smith" refer to the Pearl of Great Price.)

Most of the Book of Mormon concerns a group of people who left Jerusalem about 600 B.C. under the leadership of a prophet named Lehi. Following the Lord's directions, Lehi, his family, and one other family traveled for several years through what they called the "wilderness" (probably the Arabian Peninsula) until they came to a coastal area where the Lord commanded them to build a ship that would carry them to an unknown land "choice above all other lands." (1 Nephi 2:20.) That land was on the American continent.

Very early in their new home, the people divided into two basic groups, known as Lamanites and Nephites, and much of their subsequent history consisted of military and other tensions between the groups. The third group that came to the New World was eventually found by and assimilated into the Nephite society.

The Lamanites derived their name from Lehi's oldest son, Laman, and the Nephites from a younger son, Nephi. Nephi was the first keeper of the records and was the most prominent of all the Book of Mormon prophets. His brothers Laman and Lemuel, by contrast, were wicked and rebellious. Thus, the initial division between the Nephites and the Lamanites was essentially between the righteous and the wicked, and throughout Book of Mormon history, most of the prominent prophets and other leaders were Nephites. This was not always the case, however. Some of the significant Book of Mormon figures were Lamanites, and in the end, the Lamanites destroyed the Nephites, who had become the more wicked. The former group was among the progenitors of the American Indians.

Like other religious people who believe in the Bible, Mormons are well acquainted with Bible stories and heroes: Abraham, Joseph, Moses, Elijah, Peter, and Paul. And, in common with other Christians, Mormons believe that Jesus Christ is the most important Bible figure and the most important person who ever lived. The Old Testament predicts his coming, and the New Testament tells of his life and work.

While these biblical stories are no less important for Mormons than for other religious peoples, Mormons also have another set of scriptural stories and heroes equally fascinating and equally significant. The lives and accomplishments of Alma, Mosiah, King Benjamin, Nephi, Helaman, Samuel the Lamanite, Enos, Moroni, and Jacob are just as important to Mormons as those of the Old World prophets who received divine revelations at about the same time on the opposite side of the world. And the central person in the Book of Mormon is the same as the central person in the Bible: Jesus Christ. Indeed, the reason for the existence of the Book of Mormon is to provide another testament of Christ.

Scripture consists of the words that our Heavenly Father has given to his children through his chosen prophets. The Bible qualifies, and so does the Book of Mormon (as do the modern scriptures contained in the Doctrine and Covenants and the Pearl of Great Price). The only real difference in this respect between the Bible and the Book of Mormon is that the Book of Mormon is free from human translation errors and loss of material.

There is neither inconsistency nor tension between the Old and New Testaments. They complement and build on each other. The same is true of the relationship between the Bible and the Book of Mormon. Some biblical teachings and principles are better understood because of the Book of Mormon, but there is no tension between the two. There could not be, since both originate from the same divine source. Every major principle in the Bible concerning the Godhead and the gospel is found in the Book of Mormon, and both the Bible and the Book of Mormon teach the same plan of salvation.

Of all the biblical teachings and principles that the Book of Mormon helps to make clearer and more understandable, the ones that focus on Jesus Christ are in a class by themselves. The understanding of the divinity and mission of Jesus Christ is the primary aim of the Book of Mormon. Indeed, the complete title of the book itself is *The Book of Mormon, Another Testament for Jesus Christ.*

While discharging his stewardship in Galilee, Jesus told his followers, "Other sheep I have, which are not of this fold: them also I must bring, and they shall hear my voice; and there shall be one fold, and one shepherd." (John 10:16.) The most common assumption among Christian peoples is that Jesus was referring to the Gentiles. That is an assumption, however, at odds with the clarification by Christ himself that his mission was exclusively to the Jews: "I am not sent but unto the lost sheep of the house of Israel." (Matthew 15:24.) His disciples after him would carry his message to the Gentiles (see Acts 9:15; 10:1–48), but he himself did not. Who, then, were those other sheep, those who were not of the same fold, but who were of "the house of Israel" and who would hear his voice?

Those other sheep were the descendants of Lehi—the Nephites and Lamanites who inhabited the American continent. Following his ascension into heaven, Jesus spent a period of about forty days among those people, preaching the gospel, healing the sick, and establishing his church upon the foundation of apostles and prophets. (See 3 Nephi 11–28.) This story is told in the Book of Mormon.

The Book of Mormon prophets testified, often more plainly than did their Old Testament counterparts, of the coming and mission of Christ, teaching who he was and what he would do for us. People on this continent were baptized in his name, hundreds of years before his birth. (See Mosiah 18:8–13; Alma 16:13–14.) Even the very last words of the book are an invitation to "come unto Christ, and be perfected in him," with a promise that we will all meet before his judgment bar. (Moroni 10:32–34.) This, then, is the purpose of the book, as stated in the title page: "That they may know the covenants of the Lord, that they are not cast off forever—And also to the convincing of the Jew and Gentile that JESUS is the CHRIST, the ETERNAL GOD, manifesting himself unto all nations."

CHAPTER 3

Jesus Christ, the Son of God: Are Mormons Christian?

A question commonly asked of Mormons is whether we are Christians. I have heard the argument, at times advanced with great passion, that we are not. The argument is ridiculous. I assume that qualification as a Christian turns mainly on a belief in Christ. Mormons not only qualify as Christians under that definition, but they have also given broader meaning to the definition itself. The Restoration brought with it an understanding of Christ beyond what any other Christian sect offered. Without the principles of the restored gospel, one's understanding of Jesus Christ is less than complete, and the Savior is relegated to a lesser position than he in fact holds.

For Mormons, Jesus Christ is unique among all persons who have ever lived. He is not in a class with the biblical greats, Noah, Abraham, and Moses — he is in a class that has only one member. Mormons do not regard Jesus Christ in the same way Buddhists regard Buddha or Islamics regard Mohammed. A teacher? A role-model? A prophet? Yes, he was all of these. But history has seen others—not many, but some—who were almost in the same league as teachers, role models, and prophets.

Jesus Christ was more than a prophet. He was the one who gave instructions to the prophets. He covenanted with Abraham to bless his posterity and, through them, all the world. (See Genesis 12:1–3.) When Moses went up into the mountain and returned with the tablets of stone, the one with whom Moses spoke, who gave Moses the Ten Commandments, was the premortal Jesus Christ, Jehovah. (See Exodus 19:20–25.) And when Elijah called for a miracle to confound the priests of Baal, this same Jesus Christ, the Old Testament Jehovah, was the one who performed the miracle that Elijah requested. (See 1 Kings 18:20–39.) When Jesus showed himself to his disciples in the New World, he said: "Arise and come forth unto me, that ye may thrust your hands into my side, and also that ye may feel the prints of the nails in my hands and in my feet, that ye may know that I am the God of Israel, and the God of the whole earth, and have been slain for the sins of the world." (3 Nephi 11:14.)

Jesus Christ could easily claim that he was "God of the whole earth" because he was also the Creator, the same person who had been with God from the beginning and who had in his premortal state created the world. (See Isaiah 45:12; John 1:1.) This was accomplished under the direction of the Father, but the Son was the one who did the actual creation, as the Apostle Paul indicates: "God, who at sundry times and in divers manners spake in time past unto the fathers by the prophets, hath in these last days spoken unto us by his Son, whom he hath appointed heir of all things, by whom also he made the worlds." (Hebrews 1:1–2.) In the New World, Jesus Christ himself declared, "I created the heavens and the earth, and all things that in them are. I was with the Father from the beginning. I am in the Father, and the Father in me; and in me hath the Father glorified his name." (3 Nephi 9:15.)

Jesus Christ is also one of three separate members of the Godhead, the other two being God the Father and the Holy Ghost. Biblical statements that those three are one mean that they are unified in purpose, action, and belief, not that they are one being. This use of the word *one* is clear from Jesus' prayer to his Father for his disciples, when he said, "Neither pray I for these alone, but for them also which shall believe on me through their word; that they all may be one; as thou, Father, art in me, and I in thee, that they also may be one in us: that the world may believe that thou hast sent me. And the glory which thou gavest me I have given them; that they may be one, even as we are one: I in thee, and thou in me, that they may be made perfect in one; and that the world may know that thou hast sent me, and hast loved them, as thou hast loved me." (John 17:20–24; see also Matthew 3:13–17; 26:39; John 17:11; 1 John 5:7.)

The fact that our Heavenly Father and his Son Jesus Christ are separate individuals is another plain, simple truth that has been restored. A case can clearly be made for that from the Bible, but the events of the Restoration leave no doubt. In his first vision, Joseph Smith saw the Father and the Son. They were not a mysterious, nondescribable essence. To be sure, they were different from men in that their brightness and glory were greater than the brightness of the sun. (See

Joseph Smith–History 1:16.) But their forms were that of human beings. And there were two of them, separate and distinct.

The Father and the Son are celestial, eternal beings of flesh and bone. (See Luke 24:39.) The third member of the Godhead, the Holy Ghost, is a personage of spirit. (See D&C 130:22.) I suspect that most people who believe in God picture him as a person, anthropomorphic, one who, like our earthly fathers, looks like us. I also suspect that most people picture the Father and Son as separate beings. When God said, "Let us make man in our own image" (see Genesis 1:26), he meant what he said. The phrase "our image" was no mistake, and neither was the plural word "our." We are in the image of our Heavenly Father and his Son. They have physical bodies, though, unlike our bodies, theirs are perfect. And though they have a complete unity of purpose, their physical beings are separate and distinct.

Besides being Jehovah, Creator, and a member of the Godhead, Jesus Christ is Savior. His most important work was done in mortality. Two thousand years ago, he was born in the land of Israel, where he lived for thirty-three years. He spent thirty of those years preparing for his mission and three in carrying it out. Even if one ignores its spiritual significance, the work of that one man during those three years has had a greater effect on world history than any other work. The reason for his remarkable accomplishments is simple: Jesus Christ was the Son of God, who had power to lay down his life and take it up again. He was the literal Son of God, not only in spirit (as are all of God's children), but also in the flesh — thus he was called the only begotten

Son of God. (See Matthew 3:16–17; 17:5; John 3:16; 10:17–18.) During his years on earth, he was both God and man. Because he was God, he did not have to die, and the gift of his life was truly a voluntary act.

For this reason, his Heavenly Father sent him to earth to accomplish some things that could be accomplished only by him. Though we cannot completely understand how the Atonement works, our Savior Jesus Christ, by his suffering and his selfless acts of taking upon himself the sins of mankind and giving up his own life, atoned for both Adam's original transgression and also for our own sins. As a result, we may one day return to the presence of our Heavenly Father and his Son, our Redeemer.

Jesus Christ's atoning sacrifice, which included his crucifixion, did many things for us, the two most important being resurrection and salvation. First, when the Savior was resurrected, he broke the bands of death for everyone—he guaranteed that we will live again. This guarantee is absolute. There will be a resurrection and an afterlife for all, regardless of the kind of life a person has led on this earth. (See Job 19:26; John 5:28–29; 15:20–22; Acts 24:15; 1 Corinthians 15:20–22, 25–26.) The universal resurrection thus compensates completely for the way Adam's fall universally brought death into the world.

Second, the Savior has paid for our sins. Why is this important? Our sins, which make us unclean, separate us from God. By our own power, we cannot make ourselves clean again and bridge that separation. Furthermore, justice requires that we be punished for the divine laws we break. If left to our own devices, we would be utterly lost. But the

Atonement repairs fully the effects of our sins, if we have faith in the Savior, repent, and are baptized. (See Mark 1:4–5; Acts 2:38; 1 John 1:9.) The Savior, by his atonement, reconciles us to God. He bears the punishment for our sins and replaces our guilt with his innocence. (I discuss this further in chapter five.) Jacob, a Book of Mormon prophet, summarized the two primary benefits of the Atonement succinctly:

"He cometh into the world that he may save all men if they will hearken unto his voice; for behold, he suffereth the pains of all men, yea, the pains of every living creature, both men, women, and children, who belong to the family of Adam. And he suffereth this that the resurrection might pass upon all men, that all might stand before him at the great and judgment day. And he commandeth all men that they must repent, and be baptized in his name, having perfect faith in the Holy One of Israel, or they cannot be saved in the kingdom of God." (2 Nephi 9:21–23.)

For much of the civilized world, the birth of Jesus of Nazareth marks the point from which time itself is measured. His coming was an event foretold by Old Testament prophets and, with even greater precision, by Book of Mormon prophets. The four Gospels in the New Testament are devoted to the story of his earthly mission, during which he healed the sick, gave hope to the downtrodden, taught the principles of his gospel, established his church, and prophesied of the future. Other books in the New Testament, particularly Revelation, give us an idea of his role since his resurrection.

But without the Book of Mormon and other latter-day revelation, Christians are left without a full understanding of just how strong their case really is. Jesus Christ is more than just the central figure of the New Testament. He is also the central figure of the Old Testament: the same Jehovah, who created the world and spoke to prophets from Adam to Malachi. And this same Jesus Christ, God of the Old Testament and Redeemer of all, has once again benefited humankind by restoring the same teachings, principles, ordinances, and organization that he first brought to the world two thousand years ago.

CHAPTER 4

LIFE AND ITS PURPOSE: WHERE DID WE COME FROM? WHY ARE WE HERE? WHERE ARE WE GOING?

The Restoration provides a more complete answer to life's great questions than is available from any other source. We need not be left guessing at our origins, our purpose, and our future: Where did we come from? Why are we here? Is there anything after this life, and, if so, what is it?

The eternal human soul consists of two parts, the body and the spirit. Our bodies had their beginnings in this life. They are part of things eternal, however, because they will arise in the resurrection and reunite with the spirit. For the rest of eternity, time without end, the soul will consist of a spirit and a resurrected body. The noncorporal part of our eternal soul, the spirit, is both without beginning and without end. It has always existed, and it always will. (See D&C 93:29–30.) There was a life before this earthly one, in which we lived in the presence of our Heavenly Father, under his constant influence and subject to his guidance. Each of us was there, a separate, distinct individual, with a body whose form was like the one we now have. But it was a spirit body only. We were intelligent, thinking, feeling beings, but without bodies of flesh and bone. (See Jeremiah 1:5; Luke 24:36–43; Abraham 3:20–23.)

The answer to the first question, then, is that there was a life before this one. I was there, and you were there, though we do not remember it (for good reasons that I will deal with in a moment). Thus, our existence did not begin with live birth in this life, or nine months prior to that time, or at any point in between. We existed as spirits before this life.

Then what about the second question: Why are we here? If we lived as spirit children in the presence of our Heavenly Father, what possible reason would we have to leave such a favored state? Both the general and also the specific answers to that question are anchored in two fundamental principles of restored truth. They are eternal progression and agency.

Each of us is an eternal being. This means, literally, we will never cease to exist. Throughout our existence, we will continue to progress or retrogress. The choice is ours, both choosing to progress and choosing how fast to progress. The right to exercise the choices that will determine our progress is called agency. Just as is the case with any child in his parents' presence, there came a point in our pre-earthly existence when the very fact of being constantly in Heavenly Father's presence impeded us from further development. To continue progressing, we needed the experience of exercising our agency—making choices—under a different set of circumstances, circumstances that demanded faith. For this reason, we do not remember our Heavenly Father or the time we spent in his presence.

I have long believed that being tested outside our Heavenly Father's presence and influence is a fundamental purpose of this life. This principle provides an answer to another of life's baffling questions: Why do bad things happen to good people? For example, why would a loving Heavenly Father permit serious illness to affect some of the most decent people we know? One answer, I believe, is that the plan under which we are here necessarily places us on our own in most matters, including being susceptible to illness and disaster. If our Heavenly Father always intervened to spare the really good people from those kinds of experiences, the effect of the developmental and testing process would be blunted. In other words, if good people were spared crises, what kind of strength, resilience, faith, maturity, and wisdom would they really develop?

Though many of the things that happen to us are random experiences, there is no random or arbitrary connection between the kind of life we lead here and what will happen to us in the next life. The Lord, who was the best of us, was not spared any suffering whatsoever. But because of his suffering and sacrifice, he won not only the victory for himself, but also for all of us. The challenge God has set for us is not to be merely okay, but to be perfect as he is (see Matthew 5:48), to be like him: "It doth not yet appear what we shall be: but we know that, when he shall appear, we shall be like him" (1 John 3:2). How can that be accomplished without stretching far beyond our present selves?

But what about individual cases? Does the Lord ever intervene on behalf of an individual who is suffering or who is in danger? Does the kind of life the person has lived play any role here? And what about the efforts of the person's friends to invoke the Lord's help?

There are two ways to answer these questions. On the one hand, both the scriptures and my own personal experiences tell me that the fasting, faith, and prayers of an individual or a group of people may play a deciding role in many remarkable circumstances, such as recovery from illness. The Savior gave instructions to his original Seventy to heal the sick and to bless. (See Luke 10:1–9.) On another occasion, he pointed out that sometimes prayer alone is not enough but must be accompanied by fasting. (See Matthew 17:21.) The plain implication is that these things *do* make a difference. Similarly, there is a priesthood ordinance, used in biblical times and restored for these days, called the administration of the sick, whereby the afflicted person is anointed with oil specially consecrated for this purpose, and then given a blessing. (See James 5:14; D&C 42:43–44.)

On the other hand, while all of these things are effective, they do not always bring forth the desired result. Though many people have experienced recoveries that can only be described as miraculous, others have not improved. When terminal illness is involved, the sufferer often does not recover, even when a great many have fasted and prayed long and earnestly. In my own case, I would probably not be alive today without such efforts. But for the reasons explained previously, we cannot be assured that afflictions will always be relieved by prayer and faith; if such were the case, the fundamental premise of coming to earth to be tested would be thwarted.

It is clear to me that efforts to plead for God's help on behalf of loved ones are proper and frequently bear fruit: there are instances in which fasting, faith, prayers, and special blessings result in a person's improved health. But there are and will continue to be other instances in which those results do not occur. In either case, God furthers his overall plan "to bring to pass the immortality and eternal life of man" (Moses 1:39) by challenging individuals to develop greater faith, strength, and compassion.

Another reason for our earthly existence is to obtain bodies of flesh and bones. One of our Father's godly attributes is his ability to create life. To attain that capacity, and become more like him in that respect, we need a physical body. Furthermore, without bodies, our experience would be incomplete, and our progress would thus be impeded. With bodies, we can gain earthly experiences through the exercise of our agency, outside the presence of our Heavenly Father, and thereby pursue our eternal progression. This is a matter of degree rather than a matter of right and wrong. To give a few examples, without a body, we would have difficulty developing self-control, we would experience joy less fully, and we would not have the experience of parenthood. Our ultimate objective is complete perfection. We cannot reach this objective in this life, but the more we can do here, the greater will be our advantage following the resurrection. (See D&C 130:18–19.)

The traditional dichotomy between heaven and hell—heaven for the good and hell for the bad—has elements of truth about it. But it is too rigid and distorted. The notion that each person will be relegated either up or down, in or out, is without scriptural foundation and is quite inconsistent with a loving yet fair Father in Heaven. The Apostle Paul speaks of not just one degree of glory in the hereafter, but of three: the telestial, the terrestrial, and the celestial. (See 1 Corinthians 15:40–41.) Each of those is a heaven in the sense that a divine presence and a state of happiness will abound there, commensurate with the kinds of life we have led during our mortal testing period.

At one point the Savior told the Twelve, "In my Father's house are many mansions: if it were not so, I would have told you. I go to prepare a place for you." (John 14:2.) Within each of the three kingdoms, or degrees of glory of which Paul spoke (and which are more precisely described in D&C 76), there are further gradations. This will prevent, I believe, broad categorizations of individual lives at the day of judgment and allow justice and mercy to determine more fully and accurately our rewards.

Though eternal progression, through exercise of our agency, is an individual matter, it also affects the family because the highest goals the Lord has set for us can be achieved only as part of the eternal family unit. Our experiences in this life teach us that the greatest joys we can have are those experienced with our families: husbands and wives, children and parents, grandchildren and grandparents. Money helps to make life more pleasant. Many people find that books, VCRs, football games, music, travel, cultural performances, and jogs on a summer morning along a shaded path contribute to the quality of life. But nothing brings as much real joy as sharing those kinds of experiences with family members. Sharing them with friends may be rewarding, but friends are not in the same league as family. If some disagree with the proposition that the greatest joy is family-based, they have probably never had the kind of family relationships that contribute to such joy and richness.

The highest degree of glory cannot be achieved by any person acting alone. It is reserved for families—husband and wife and children. And it is not available to all families whose members live good lives and love each other. What is needed in addition are certain priesthood ordinances that the Lord has declared essential for salvation.

A key element of the eternal plan is the making of choices, and among the crucial choices is the acceptance of particular ordinances, one of which is baptism. Jesus clearly taught this (see John 3:3–5, 22), as did his apostles (see Acts 2:38). The baptizing done by John the Baptist was for a purpose, and the fact that the Savior of the world was baptized shows that it was more than just a symbol people are free to accept or reject. The reason the Lord gave for his baptism was "to fulfil all righteousness." (Matthew 3:15.)

Another important priesthood ordinance is eternal marriage. No other marriage ceremony performed by any other authority even purports to last beyond the grave. The familiar phrase "until death do us part" is significant. Earthly marriage ceremonies are exactly what they say they are: valid for the term of this life, and nothing beyond. Eternal marriage opens the way for a marriage to continue in the hereafter.

The only place such an ordinance can be performed is

in one of the temples. Mormon temples are not places where members meet once a week for devotional and instructional purposes; those buildings are called chapels. Temples are fewer in number, and their principal purpose is for the performance of certain sacred ordinances. Members who have a temple recommend may enter the temple. A temple recommend is a small certificate issued by the member's immediate ecclesiastical leaders — the bishop and stake president — after interviews determine that the person is an active member of the Church and keeps the basic commandments (discussed in chapter six).

A marriage solemnized in one of the Lord's holy temples lasts forever if the couple stay righteous. The marriage literally never ends. It preserves forever what most happily married couples would agree is the most important thing they have: their family relationship. This is broader than the relationship between husband and wife, for it includes the entire family: parents with their children, and brothers and sisters with each other. If the children of a couple married eternally also marry in the temple, the bond expands to include grandparents with their grandchildren, and on and on for each generation who marry eternally.

In addition to the effect it has on the afterlife, eternal marriage has rather practical consequences for this life. I have a different perspective toward my family members because I understand that the relationships I have with them will exist for more than a few decades. The spiritual and intellectual progress the members of my family make, the degree of happiness that we feel about being a family, and the extent to which each of us derives genuine joy from the happiness of other family members not only constitute building blocks for the hereafter, but also contribute to the pleasantness of life on this earth.

More particularly, it gives me a different perspective about my children. I know, for instance, that the younger ones who now struggle with rather elementary levels of learning will one day have an understanding that equals and, in some respects, exceeds that of mine and my wife's understanding. Together, through eternity, side by side with my wife, bonded to our children and their spouses and to their children and to their children's children, we will grow and progress in knowledge and in our love and appreciation for each other and for a loving Father and his Son whose plan has made these things possible. During his earthly ministry, the Savior gave his apostles the power to seal on earth and in heaven (see Matthew 16:19; 18:18), and in these last days, that same power has been restored (see D&C 1:8; 27:12; 110:13–16; 124:93; 132:45–47) to bless our lives and our purpose for living.

CHAPTER 5

SAVED BY FAITH
OR GOOD WORKS?
GRACE AND THE
PLAN OF SALVATION

On which side do Mormons align themselves in the great debate over faith versus works? Do we agree with Paul that "for by grace are [we] saved through faith, and that not of [ourselves]: it is the gift of God: not of works, lest any man should boast"? (Ephesians 2:8–9; see also Romans 3:24–28; Galatians 2:16.) Or do we side with James's pronouncement that "faith without works is dead" and that "by works a man is justified, and not by faith only"? (James 2:20, 24; see Matthew 16:27.)

We understand that both are correct. Properly understood, there is no contradiction between the two claims. First, we are saved *by grace*. We cannot save ourselves; our own efforts alone cannot turn us into exalted beings or make us like the Father and the Son. The mercy and love of God have been extended to us to do for us what we cannot do for ourselves: specifically, cleanse us, make us holy and innocent, resurrect us, and glorify us. That is grace—what the Lord does for us because of his goodwill toward us, not because we merit it.

Second, we are saved by grace *through faith*. We are also saved by grace *through works,* because we know that where there are no works, there is no faith. James's point in his discussion of faith and works is that they are inseparable. He said, "By works was faith made perfect." (James 2:22.) Paul did not teach faith only (faith without works) but noted the importance of works in the eyes of God: "He became the author of eternal salvation unto all them that obey him." (Hebrews 5:9.) "[God] will render to every man according to his deeds: to them who by patient continuance in well doing, seek for glory and honour and immortality, eternal life: but unto them that are contentious, and do not obey the truth, but obey unrighteousness, indignation and wrath, tribulation and anguish, upon every soul of man that doeth evil. . . . For not the hearers of the law are just before God, but the doers of the law shall be justified." (Romans 2:6–9, 13; see also Matthew 20:21–23; Mark 10:36–40.)

Many aspects of God's grace are unconditional. For instance, one free gift of salvation is resurrection and immortality, given by Jesus Christ to all people who have lived on this earth. This gift is not affected by anything we do here. Everyone, from the most righteous to the most wretched, will be resurrected and will live forever in the next life. (See 1 Corinthians 15:20–22; Alma 40:4; Alma 11:41–44; D&C 29:26.) By breaking the bands of death, Jesus Christ overcame death, and all will live again. In this respect, we are saved by grace unconditionally.

The fall of Adam and Eve also barred us from the Lord's presence — it separated us from Jesus Christ. One universal gift from the Savior is to bring us back to his presence. This will be done at what is called the judgment day, when all will stand before Christ to be judged of their sins. (See Revelation 20:11–13; Moroni 10:27, 34.) This aspect of grace is also unconditional, though undoubtedly many will not relish the experience.

Another aspect of God's grace is his offer of mercy — he will satisfy the demands of justice for us if we accept him and the gospel covenant. This offer is universal; all may receive this gift: "He inviteth them all to come unto him and partake of his goodness; and he denieth none that come unto him, black and white, bond and free, male and female; and he remembereth the heathen; and all are alike unto God, both Jew and Gentile. (2 Nephi 26:33; see also Isaiah 55:1–3.) The degree of glory that we will enjoy depends not on whether we happen to be one of the lucky ones to whom a celestial wheel of fortune has given a high number. Rather, he offers forgiveness to all who repent and are faithful.

To say we have faith and not do what the Lord asks is hypocritical. Likewise, to do good works and yet not believe is also hypocritical. What is it, then, that the Lord asks of us to show our acceptance of his offer of salvation? The answer to that question begins with what Joseph Smith called the first four principles and ordinances of the gospel: faith in Jesus Christ, repentance, baptism by immersion for the remission of sins, and the laying on of hands for the gift of the Holy Ghost. All four are principles, and the final two are ordinances. (An ordinance can be defined as an action —

or an act — performed by someone with priesthood authority for someone else.)

Faith in Jesus Christ certainly deserves its ranking as the first principle of the gospel. Paul defined faith as "the substance [Greek, assurance] of things hoped for, the evidence of things not seen." (Hebrews 11:1.) It is a process for gaining understanding beyond that gained through human intelligence. We believe that it is compatible with rational processes, and indeed, the two, working in tandem, provide the most complete means by which humans can attain understanding. Thus, modern scripture admonishes that we should gain knowledge by study and also by faith. (See D&C 88:118.)

Faith is particularly essential to a religion whose foundational tenets include revelation and restoration of priesthood authority. While the intellectual and spiritual processes complement rather than exclude each other, only through faith can one really come to understand the things of God. The intellectual, inductive approach simply will not work. That is, if one undertakes to determine the truthfulness of Mormonism by first listing the various points of doctrine and then asking whether, as a rational matter, he agrees or disagrees with each of them, he will probably come up with a fairly satisfactory but not a conclusive answer. Chances are he will agree on most matters, perhaps disagree on a few, and be uncertain as to several.

For instance, the only real way to reach a bottom line yes or no with respect to the restoration issue is to start with the bottom line itself: Did Joseph Smith really have the experiences that he said he had? Is the Book of Mormon really the work of a series of prophets to whom God revealed his word in ancient times? Have our Heavenly Father and his Son Jesus Christ restored all things, including apostles and prophets? Those are matters that can be resolved only through the processes of faith—excercising a belief and living a principle in such a way that they will bring a response through the Holy Ghost from God. If there are individual matters that I do not understand, I know that my lack of understanding reflects only on my ability to understand and not on whether or not the Restoration truly happened.

So it is with good reason that faith is the first principle of the gospel. Properly understood, no real dichotomy exists between faith and works, because faith itself is a work. Unlike the concept of grace, something we simply receive or do not receive according to someone else's whim or pleasure, faith and its fruits depend on our willingness to engage in real effort. Among its fruits are increased knowledge and understanding of things eternal, things of everlasting and foundational significance. They include convictions that Jesus Christ is the literal son of God; that he is the Creator and Savior of the world; that once again in these last days he has restored to the earth the same gospel, same organization, and same truths that he announced two millennia ago when he was physically on earth; and that pursuant to that restoration, he has once again placed prophets among us through whom he reveals his will, just as in olden times.

Such convictions, acquired through faith, do not come about by patiently and passively waiting for them to descend upon us, or hoping that they will. They require positive effort on our part—conscientious effort. Recall the admonition of Moroni in the Book of Mormon, chapter ten, verse four: "When ye shall receive these things, I would exhort you that ye would ask God, the Eternal Father, in the name of Christ, if these things are not true; and if ye shall ask with a sincere heart, with real intent, having faith in Christ, he will manifest the truth of it unto you, by the power of the Holy Ghost."

In short, it is not a choice of either faith or works. The two are integral parts of a single whole, and, for reasons stated above, the writings of both Paul and James show this. Faith is the foundation on which we build, but it is not a foundation that springs into full-blown existence by pure chance.

The second principle, *repentance,* means turning away from a sin and turning toward righteousness. Forsaking sin involves both an emotional and a physical break from transgression, giving rise to sorrow and regret. It also involves trying to repair the damage done by one's sins, as far as that is possible. Thus, in many instances, confession is necessary, as in going to a person one has wronged and confessing one's wrongdoing. The marvelous thing about repentance is forgiveness. Not only may we obtain forgiveness from others, but more important, God himself will forgive us. In this light, repentance is adequately understood only in conjunction with the third principle, *baptism.*

Baptism is not just an optional formality by which a person signifies an interest in acquiring a formal affiliation with the Church. The Savior of the world made it quite clear that baptism is a prerequisite to exaltation. (See John 3:5; Mark 16:16; Alma 7:14.) It is, therefore, one of the works without which faith is dead. One purpose of baptism, as the New Testament abundantly testifies, is the cleansing of sin, and this process is inextricably linked with the principle of repentance.

Repentance—a conscientious effort to cure one's faults, sins, and misdeeds and to refrain from recommitting them in the future—is, initially, a prerequisite to baptism. Baptism then symbolically and literally washes away those sins. Other transgressions of varying types and degrees will inevitably recur after baptism. Only one person in the history of the world was perfect. Baptism, however, is effective not only for the purpose of cleansing one's sins at the time the ordinance was performed, but also enables the individual, through repentance, to be forgiven and cleansed of other transgressions committed after baptism. For that reason, though misdeeds recur following baptism, there is no need for the ordinance to be performed again. The subsequent cleansing process can be accomplished through repentance, with the benefit of the initial baptism.

The scriptures, both biblical and modern, make it very clear that baptism is required and that the Savior himself instituted it. The scriptures are also very clear that the proper method of baptism is by immersion: "Buried with him in baptism, wherein ye are also risen with him." (Colossians 2:12; see also Matthew 3:16.) "Then shall ye immerse them in the water, and come forth again out of the water. And after this manner shall ye baptize in my name." (3 Nephi 11:26–27.) "They [the just] are they who received the testimony of Jesus, and believed on his name and were baptized after the manner of his burial, being buried in the water in his name, and this according to the commandment which he has given." (D&C 76:51.)

Symbolically, this makes sense. Paul points out that baptism is like a new birth. It is a type of the crucifixion and resurrection: the old man of sin is destroyed, and we come out of the water, reborn into a newness of life. (See Romans 6:4; see also Mosiah 27:25; D&C 5:16.) Similarly, immersion is symbolically faithful to the concept of complete washing away of sins.

Because baptism is for the remission of sins, infant baptism is unnecessary and improper. No one could imagine that an infant sins. (In addition, if one accepts immersion as the proper means of baptism, infant baptism could be quite dangerous.) The Prophet Mormon decried infant baptism as wrong. (See Moroni 8:10–11; D&C 20:71, 29:46–47, 93:38.) Through modern revelation, the Lord has made it known that one reaches accountability, and therefore becomes eligible for baptism, when he reaches the age of eight. (See D&C 68:27.)

For a Mormon, baptism is one of two or three of life's most important events. For the hundreds of thousands of people who are converted to the Church each year, it is a symbol of a new way of life, of a commitment to and an acceptance of the restored gospel. It is also a landmark event for the person who has grown up as a member of a Mormon family. At age eight, the child is capable of understanding the basic principles of the gospel and the basic purposes of baptism and of knowing the essential difference between right and wrong, between things that are important and things that are not so important. For several years prior, that child will have received an abundant education concerning both the meaning and the significance of baptism and will have been anticipating this important event.

The fourth principle of the gospel is the *laying on of hands for the gift of the Holy Ghost*. It refers to an ordinance following baptism, in which the recently baptized person is confirmed a member of the Church and promised the continuing assistance of the Holy Ghost in making decisions and conducting one's life after baptism. The shorthand name for that ordinance is confirmation. Both the ordinance and the office and function of the Holy Ghost have deep biblical roots. The Holy Ghost is the third member of the Godhead, a personage separate and distinct from the Father and the Son. Unlike the other two, however, he is a personage of spirit. (See D&C 130:22.) The Book of Mormon tells us that his form is that of a man, though his substance is spirit. (See 1 Nephi 11:11.) During his time on earth, the Savior made numerous references to the Holy Ghost, who would be a comforter following the Savior's departure. (See John 14: 15–17.)

Very simply, through the influence of the Holy Ghost, mortals can come to an understanding of what is true and what is not. This influence is manifest in two different ways. Prior to baptism, those who earnestly seek it are blessed with this influence for the purpose of gaining an understanding. This occurred, for example, in the case of the multitudes who gathered on the Day of Pentecost to hear Peter speak (see Acts 2), and again in the case of Cornelius, the centurion, the first non-Jew to receive the gospel in New Testament times (see Acts 10). Note, however, that those who were converted by the influence of the Holy Ghost on the day of Pentecost asked Peter and the other apostles, "Men and brethren, what shall we do?" (Acts 2:37.) Peter's response was "Repent, and be baptized every one of you in the name of Jesus Christ for the remission of sins, and ye shall receive the gift of the Holy Ghost." (Acts 2:38.)

What does this mean? If those converts had already come under the influence of the Holy Ghost, why would they then, following baptism, have any need to "receive the gift of the Holy Ghost"? The differences between the effect of the Holy Ghost before and after confirmation are largely differences of permanence and of degree. Those who earnestly seek the Holy Ghost's assistance before baptism for the purpose of knowing the truth will receive that assistance. Indeed, such assistance is essential to the conversion process. The promise that one receives through the ordinance following baptism is a promise that the Holy Ghost will be one's constant companion, if one lives worthily of such a blessing.

Unlike baptism, which can be performed by one holding the Aaronic, or lesser, Priesthood, confirmation is performed only by a person holding the Melchizedek, or greater, Priesthood. Confirmation does not guarantee the constant companionship of the Holy Ghost, and unless one lives worthily to receive the benefits, it is worthless. But if one does live worthily, he or she is entitled to have the Holy Ghost as a companion. This companionship provides greater access to an understanding of the things that we should be doing with our lives, greater sensitivity not just to the difference between right and wrong, but to gradations of rightness and goodness: What ought to be our emphasis or our focus?

SAVED BY FAITH OR GOOD WORKS?

What kinds of things will bring the greatest happiness to ourselves and our families and the most significant progress toward eventual perfection?

Beyond the first four principles and ordinances, there is a broad range of good works — activities and service — in which we should be involved, ranging from some that are very general to some that are rather specific. Clearly the most important are the ones that the Savior described as the first two great commandments: "Thou shalt love the Lord thy God" and "Thou shalt love thy neighbour as thyself." (Matthew 22:36–40; see also 2 Nephi 31:20; Moroni 10:32.) As the Lord pointed out, all other commandments are really included within these two. Those two mandates, to love our Heavenly Father and to love our fellow human beings, are the beacon lights toward which we should all continuously move.

The one that really tests the difference between theory and practice is the second great commandment, to love others as ourselves. I take that commandment as a literal one. I believe that ultimate perfection, the final step in our eternal progress, will be achieved when the well-being of every other person is literally just as important as is our own. Aside from the Savior himself, no one on this earth has ever achieved that objective in this life. But we have an eternity in which to work on it, plus the benefit of the Savior's enabling power, and there is no better measurement (though the measuring process is very difficult) of a true adherent to the restored gospel than the extent of that person's concern for other people.

Aside from the two great commandments and the first

four principles, there are other, more specific, examples of "good works" that rank high in the Mormon hierarchy of values. These patterns of living, which involve practices that, in the eyes of some, identify the Mormon life-style, will be discussed in the following chapter.

CHAPTER 6

"KEEP THE COMMANDMENTS" — MORMONISM AND MORALS

In the press conference following his ordination as eleventh President of the Church, President Harold B. Lee was asked what message he wanted to deliver to the members. His response, "Keep the commandments. There could be nothing that I could say that would be a more powerful or important message today." (*Ensign,* August 1972, p. 20.)

This was a message that the members would understand. They knew what he meant by "the commandments." Certainly he meant the two great commandments, the ten commandments, and the first four principles of the gospel. They also clearly knew that he had in mind additional, specific commandments that are important to Mormons. Some of these are discussed in the following pages, not necessarily in order of importance.

Sexual Morality. Marital fidelity and a complete absence of sexual intercourse outside the bonds of marriage rank very high in the Mormon scheme of values. In terms of overt, objectively identifiable conduct, few if any misdeeds are more serious than extramarital sexual intercourse. Adultery is something that a good Mormon simply should not do or even consider, because it not only offends the scriptural sexual rules, but also does so in a way that adversely affects the family. Quite simply, the person who commits adultery is not a good Mormon—he or she has put himself away from the Church, becoming subject to excommunication or disfellowship. The scriptures also explain that fornication is wrong. This means that sexual intercourse in premarital relationships, including between potential marriage partners, is a sin.

Our views concerning adultery and sexual promiscuity reflect more generally our views that the Lord was really serious about the commandments given in the Bible. Except for those commandments that the Lord himself has told us we are no longer obligated to live (such as some of the Old Testament dietary rules), the biblical commandments are still in force. And that includes the seventh of the Ten Commandments. The principles of sexual abstinence before marriage and sexual fidelity after marriage were true in biblical times. They are just as true today.

We believe that there are good sociological reasons for our Heavenly Father's rule against marital infidelity. We believe that loyalty in all things between marriage partners, including sexual relationships, leads to trust and to happier marriages and families. But those are not issues that good Mormons resolve for themselves based in any way on sociological or psychological considerations. Marital fidelity and the avoidance of premarital sexual relationships are commandments that come from the Lord. They are not to be debated. Each member is not free to reach his or her own conclusion as to whether the seventh commandment should be obeyed. Every member, to be sure, should try to understand the reasons for this or any other commandment. And in this instance, I submit that the conclusion is a fairly easy one to reach. But in any event, the biblical injunctions against adultery and fornication are not something the faithful Mormon will ignore.

Profanity. We also take seriously the other provisions of the Ten Commandments, including one greatly disregarded today: "Thou shalt not take the name of the Lord thy God in vain." (Exodus 20:7.) Firmly ingrained in Mormon culture is an abhorrence of taking the Lord's name in vain. Many people in American society and in other societies use the names of both the Father and the Son as expletives or even epithets. You may have noticed that your good Mormon friends will not use the name of deity, either the Father or the Son, except in a religious, reverential context. The reason is the explicit prohibition of the third commandment. Like the seventh, this one has not been repealed, and we take it seriously. Our respect for our Heavenly Father and his Son, our Savior, demands no less.

The Sabbath Day. We are also quite traditional in our observance of the Sabbath day (in our society, perhaps the most disregarded commandment of all). However, in contrast to adultery and respect for the name of deity, there is a range of views among members of the Church as to what should be done and what should not be done on the Sabbath. There is, however, universal agreement on the core proposition that the Sabbath is a day different from any other. It

51

is a day that belongs to the Lord. It is to be treated differently in the things that we do and in the degree of attention that we give things spiritual. On that day, we should turn our attention to our Heavenly Father, his Son, and the things that they taught.

There is a minimum in regard to the Sabbath day that virtually all active Church members would agree on. It is attendance at sacrament meeting, one of a three-hour block of meetings held every Sunday. The sacrament meeting derives its name and its importance from the ordinance of the sacrament, which the members participate in during this meeting. Partaking first of broken bread and then of water as part of an ordinance have historical roots reaching back to the Savior's last supper before his crucifixion. (See Luke 22:19–20.) The bread and the water are symbolic of his flesh and blood, and each member's participation in the sacrament is a renewal of the covenants that he or she made at the time of baptism. The sacrament meeting, which also includes talks given by Church members, hymns, and an opening and closing prayer, lasts a little over an hour.

The remainder of the three-hour period is devoted to various classes and meetings. The children under twelve years of age spend two hours in Primary, meeting together for songs and talks and dividing into classes according to age. The other members attend Sunday School classes for an hour. The remaining hour is spent in priesthood classes for the men, in a Relief Society class for women eighteen and older (Relief Society is the name of the Church organization for women), and in Young Women classes for women twelve to eighteen.

As with so many other commandments, keeping the Sabbath day holy has ancient roots. After six days, or time periods, in which the Lord created the earth, he rested on the seventh and blessed it as a day of rest. He reaffirmed the uniqueness and sacredness of one day in seven by including the Sabbath as one of the Ten Commandments. These origins, plus the purpose of setting the Sabbath aside as a day different from other days of the week, mean that Sunday is a time to avoid gainful employment. So also are the usual forms of recreation. Most Church members would agree that patronizing theaters, movies, and sporting events outside of the home are not appropriate on the Sabbath. There is less agreement, however, about watching television and engaging in other common activities around the home.

The avoidance of laying down strictures on what is and what is not appropriate for the Sabbath is related to the point Jesus himself made when he harvested corn on the Sabbath and pointed out that the Sabbath is made for man and not man for the Sabbath. (See Mark 2:27.) A favorite saying among Church members is this one used by the Savior: if your ox is in a pit on the Sabbath, get him out. (See Luke 14:5.)

Why do we celebrate the Sabbath on Sunday instead of Saturday, which is, after all, the seventh day of the week? The Lord rested on the seventh day of creation, not the first, and the Latin word from which "Saturday" derives means Sabbath. The answer is quite simple. Up until the resurrection of Jesus Christ, the Sabbath was observed on the seventh day. But the early Christians began to meet on the first day of the week in commemoration of the Lord's resurrection (see Acts 20:7; 1 Corinthians 16:2), and Mormons, along with the majority of present-day Christian denominations, do likewise.

The Word of Wisdom. If you were to ask a randomly selected sample of people what they know about Mormons, one of the first responses you would likely hear is that we do not smoke or drink alcohol. The general impression is a correct one. And like the commandment against adultery and using the Lord's name in vain, we do not fudge on this one. Taking a rare social drink or smoking an occasional after-dinner cigar—on any occasion for any purpose in any amount—are simply not the kinds of things a serious Mormon would even consider.

Health-based practices as a matter of religious observance can be traced to Old Testament times (see Leviticus 11; Daniel 1:8–16), but the source of the Mormon practice is modern. It is defined in the eighty-ninth section of the Doctrine and Covenants. That section specifically prohibits the consumption of tobacco, alcohol, and hot drinks, which early Church leaders identified as coffee and tea, and gives us the phrase "Word of Wisdom" by which the commandment is known. (For Mormons, the term thus has a meaning different from what the words would literally imply.)

The Word of Wisdom is more than just a commandment about health. It is both "a principle with promise" (D&C 89:3) and a practice that identifies a person as one of the modern-day children of Israel. Some may argue, for instance, that a small amount of alcohol taken at some intervals apart causes absolutely no harm to one's health. Similarly, some believe that consuming many of today's junk foods is more harmful to the body than tea and coffee. Whether either of these views is correct is quite irrelevant. The Word of Wisdom's commandment is not to restrict one's intake to certain quantities and circumstances that are deemed safe. It is to leave them alone entirely. And while section eighty-nine also admonishes the wise use of herbs, fruit, meats, and grains, four things are in a category by themselves. The serious Mormon does not smoke or drink alcohol, tea, and coffee because the Lord has commanded him or her not to drink or smoke. In return, the Lord has promised to grant us blessings of health and wisdom and recognize us as his disciples. (See D&C 89:18–21.)

Tithing and Other Financial Obligations. Being an active Mormon is not cheap. Another of the Biblical commands that has never been repealed (and whose importance, in fact, has been reaffirmed by modern scripture) is the payment of tithing. (See Genesis 28:22; Luke 18:12.) The concept is quite simple. The Lord blesses us with many things, including our incomes, and he asks ten percent in return. Historically, tithing was usually paid "in kind" — eggs, squash, corn, potatoes, along with cash when it was available; nowadays, tithing is typically based on monetary income. Tithing was a practice of the Israelites in the Old and New Testaments, and for Mormons, being a full tithe payer is an important and integral part of Church membership. Like observance of the Ten Commandments, it is not an optional practice or something that the Church member pays now and then. If you are a believing, practicing Mormon, you pay tithing.

Tithing is the largest element of a Church member's

financial contribution, but it is not the only one. Fast offerings and other welfare contributions are used to care for the needs of the poor, principally the needy members of the Church. The fast offering is given the first Sunday of every month, which is a day of fasting for all Church members, and it generally amounts to at least the equivalent of what a family would have spent on the two meals it doesn't eat that Sunday. As with tithing, fasting and fast offerings have ancient scriptural foundations. (See 1 Kings 21:9; Nehemiah 9:1; Joel 1:14.) Through fasting once a month and on other special occasions, we believe that we draw closer to our Heavenly Father.

In recent years, many Church members have keyed fast-offering contributions to a more generous standard than the value of fasting for two meals. The most effective way to share the financial property we enjoy with less-prosperous brothers and sisters worldwide is through payment of generous fast offerings. These funds are used exclusively to care for the needy.

There is one other short-term but major financial obligation. Families who are supporting either their own children or others as missionaries can expect to pay a monthly amount during the time the missionary serves — at this time, two years for men, one-and-a-half years for women, and six months to two years for older couples. The missionary department of the Church has determined the average cost per missionary — currently $350 per month for each missionary — and distributes the collected missionary funds throughout the world. Each family supporting a missionary pays the Church-wide average.

The total annual financial obligation for the active Mormon exceeds ten percent of his income. That is a lot of money. Do Mormons regard this as an onerous burden? I know this may surprise the reader, and I can see the eyebrows rising in disbelief, but I am convinced that the overwhelming majority of tithe payers not only do not resent or wish they did not have to pay tithing, they in fact derive genuine satisfaction from it. How can this be? Let me offer several perspectives:

The first is that the experiences of Church members are replete with stories of financial blessings that have come at crucial times to full tithe payers. I am personally not certain about the directness of the link between my payment of tithing and my own financial welfare. But I believe that there is a general connection, though not in all cases dollar for dollar. Certainly that conclusion is consistent with the challenge and promise of the Lord in Malachi 3:10: "Bring ye all the tithes into the storehouse, that there may be meat in mine house, and prove me now herewith, saith the Lord of hosts, if I will not open you the windows of heaven, and pour you out a blessing, that there shall not be room enough to receive it."

The second perspective is that regardless of the link between the payment of tithing and financial welfare, tithing is a commandment. It is one of those ancient commandments that has been reinstituted through the restoration of all things. Since I am absolutely convinced that the Restoration is a reality, I am grateful for this clarification that the Lord has given me concerning the nature and the extent of what is expected of me financially.

A third and closely related point is that because the Church is the restored kingdom of God, the message of its restoration is the most important message to come to earth in the last two thousand years. Knowing that fact, I want to do what I can to make that information available to other people. While I have some nonfinancial obligations and opportunities for service in that respect, one of the easiest and most efficient ways for me to contribute to the building of the kingdom is to make financial contributions that can then be used to construct buildings; support missionary work, welfare programs, and Church educational institutions; and otherwise pay the expenses incurred by a rapidly growing church, especially one that is expanding phenomenally in countries much poorer than the United States.

Welfare. The Church operates an extensive welfare system that attempts to care for the needs of the poor, and each active member participates in the program through fast offerings, which was discussed earlier, and volunteer service. The ultimate objective of the program is to develop self-reliance in those who receive assistance so they may become self-supporting. The principal beneficiaries of this welfare program are needy Church members. As part of the program, the Church has properties that produce and manufacture a broad range of food and other items essential to a minimal standard of living. Much of the labor needed to operate and service these properties is donated by Church members, with wards and stakes (the designations for local Church units) taking turns providing manpower to run them. Like others of my faith, I have spent many hours building fences on a Church welfare cattle ranch, picking fruit, thinning sugar beets, and removing manure from a dairy farm. Others can peanut butter, package noodle products, pick cotton, make soap, grow corn, and participate in hundreds of other projects.

Distribution of goods is administered through local congregations, called wards. The bishop, who is the presiding officer of the ward, and the Relief Society president assess needs after meeting with an individual or the adult members of the family. (The Relief Society—whose motto is "Charity Never Faileth"—is the oldest women's organization in the United States, and each ward has its own Relief Society organization.) The recipients of assistance will pay back the cost of the aid by working on the welfare properties and reimbursing the ward after they regain financial independence.

The Mormon's first welfare responsibility is to care for the needs of his and her own family. This means two things. First, families work to have a reserve of food, clothing, and other resources that family members can draw on in times of need. Second, where needs exceed the immediate family's ability to provide, members turn to other relatives before turning to the general Church's resources.

Family Home Evening. Both in its doctrine and in its practices, the Mormon church is family oriented. We believe that the family is the basic ecclesiastical unit in this life, and that families as well as individuals will continue through eternity. Mormon families pray together as a family. Many also read and discuss the scriptures together on some kind of a regular basis. Probably the best-known feature of Mormon family life is the weekly home evening, usually held on Monday evening (no other church activities are scheduled on this night). The content of these weekly family home evenings varies, ranging from lessons, to family talent nights, to game nights, or to some activity inside or outside the home. Family home evening belongs to the family, and it is used for something that its members find useful and enjoyable as a family. Properly used, it significantly unifies and solidifies the family.

Home and Visiting Teaching. A central feature of Mormon practice is that members of each ward, which consists of about 100–150 families, are assigned to teach each other every month in the homes. There are two basic programs. The first, called home teaching, is carried out by the priesthood. Each family is visited briefly, perhaps for fifteen to thirty minutes, by a pair of priesthood holders, one of whom may be a young man fourteen or above. Their responsibility is to help care for the general well-being and needs of the family. During their monthly visits, the home teachers may deliver a special message from the bishop or any other message they think appropriate. This individual care greatly facilitates the bishop's responsibilities, for home teachers can call on the resources of the ward through the bishop; otherwise, the bishop would often be ignorant of the many spiritual, financial, emotional, and social problems that arise. Whenever a family wants help, they should feel free to ask their home teachers. In an effectively functioning ward, the home teachers are the ones to whom individuals or families turn in the first instance when help is needed.

The other monthly teaching program, called visiting teaching, is carried out by the women of the ward for the women in the ward. The program is administered through the Relief Society, and the women teach each other in the home. Their lessons focus on things pertaining to the family and the home and attempt to meet women's needs. Visiting teachers also render compassionate service that ranges from financial and other welfare assistance to comfort and help in the home in cases of illness or other family difficulty.

That brings us to one of the greatest commandments of the Church, one given by Jesus Christ to his disciples after his resurrection: "Go ye therefore, and teach all nations, baptizing them in the name of the Father, and of the Son, and of the Holy Ghost: teaching them to observe all things whatsoever I have commanded you." (Matthew 28:19–20.) We feel that this commandment is as important today as when it was first given. It will be discussed in the next chapter.

CHAPTER 7

PREACHING THE GOSPEL:
THE MISSIONARIES AND THE
MISSIONARY SYSTEM

You have probably heard of the Mormon missionaries. Chances are good that you have seen them on the street or in your neighborhood. Or they may have knocked on your door or contacted you some other way. They always go in pairs, and you usually can't mistake them for anyone else. The young men carry scriptures and wear distinctive white shirts, dark pants, dark ties, and name tags. The young women wear modest dresses or skirts and blouses, and they too have name tags and carry scriptures. Beyond this, the missionaries carry an aura of youthful optimism and enthusiasm unique to their calling. When you see them, you know who they are and what they are doing.

By the end of 1992, approximately forty-four thousand of these missionaries were serving in all fifty states and more than one hundred and thirty territories and foreign countries. All serve at their own expense (most of which is borne by the family). As mentioned previously, the men presently serve for two years, the women for one-and-a-half years, and the couples for up to two years, though the standard lengths of missions have varied in the past.

From the beginning, missionary efforts have been an integral part of the work of Jesus Christ's church, including, interestingly enough, the practice of sending out missionaries in pairs. (See Luke 10:1; Acts 11:30; 12:25; 15:39–40.) The natural link between our Savior's church and missionary work is dictated by the very nature of the Savior's message, both what was preached in his time and what has been restored in our time. The ancient and modern gospel of Jesus Christ consists of principles that come directly from the Savior himself. Necessarily, those who are aware of his message have an obligation to share it with others. (See Matthew 24:14; 28:19.)

The primary objective of missionary work is not simply to add numbers to existing membership lists. For example, missionaries in Mexico and other Latin American countries have for decades converted several times as many people a year per missionary as those in France or Germany or some other parts of Europe. A corporate sales manager faced with consistently better performance in one area than in another would shift his resources to concentrate on the more productive area. And I suppose that Church leaders have given some attention in the past decades to the relationship between results and number of missionaries. Significantly though, the effort has never stopped, and never will stop, for areas with relatively few conversions. We believe the gospel must be preached to all nations, not just the most receptive ones.

In April 1830 Samuel Smith, a younger brother of the Prophet Joseph, undertook one of the first missionary efforts after the organization of the Church. Armed with a few copies of their recently published Book of Mormon, Brother Smith spent approximately sixteen days traveling through Livingston and Ontario counties in New York State. He concluded that he had been a failure since he hadn't converted anyone. Subsequent events proved otherwise. The copies of the Book of Mormon he distributed eventually found their way to Brigham Young and Heber C. Kimball, who later became two of the most prominent Church leaders of the last half of the nineteenth century. Indeed, Brigham Young succeeded Joseph Smith as prophet and President of the Church. He served longer in that position than any other man. During most of his tenure as President, Heber C. Kimball was his first counselor.

The early missionary efforts of 1829 and 1830, such as Samuel Smith's proselyting journey, have continued unabated to the present time. Missionary work has always been a constant and inseparable feature of the restored gospel. Every member of the Church, regardless of age or status in life, is expected to share the gospel with others.

The heart of the missionary effort, however, remains with the men and women who devote their full time during the period of their missionary service exclusively to this work. In almost all cases, those who want to serve full-time missions initiate the process themselves. The local bishop and stake president determine worthiness and fitness of the prospective missionary to serve, and they send to the Church missionary department the necessary paperwork and their recommendations. The Church missionary department reviews the material, and the First Presidency of the Church issues the mission call to the individual.

The call to serve in a particular part of the world results from inspiration either to the First Presidency or other General Authorities acting on their behalf. The only certainty is that the missionary will not be called to serve close to his or her home. Because the calls are the product of inspiration, language capacity is not a determining factor. Thus, it is not uncommon for a Latin American to be sent to Japan, or a German to Brazil, or a Czech to Utah. Prior to actual entry into an area of service, the missionary receives formal training at a Missionary Training Center (MTC), the largest of which is located in Provo, Utah, near the Brigham Young University campus owned and operated by the Church. Typically, the MTC training period lasts eight weeks for those called to a foreign-language mission and two weeks for those who will be speaking their own language.

During their service, missionaries do not date or visit their families. They are supervised by an appointed leader who, with his wife, is called for three years to preside as president over a particular geographic area, called a "mission." Their service, like that of the missionaries, is voluntary. Only their expenses are paid. As of July 1992, there were 277 missions: 130 were English-speaking, 71 were Spanish-speaking, and the rest were spread through countries in which 23 languages dominate. In 1991 and 1992 alone, new missions were opened in 19 countries. (See "Missions, Temples," *Deseret News 1993–1994 Church Almanac* [Salt Lake City: Deseret News, 1992].)

During the period of missionary service, the parents, often assisted by the missionary's savings and by donations from relatives, friends, and ward members, typically contribute to the Church's missionary funds an amount equal to the average worldwide cost of $350 a month to sustain a missionary. The Church organization then handles financial disbursement to the individual missions and missionaries. Families welcome the responsibility to support their missionaries because of the spiritual growth and unity that result. In a way, the entire family participates in a mission through prayers, letters, and financial support.

Many people who have inquired about my own experiences as a missionary seem to be impressed that I willingly devoted two of the most productive years of my life to voluntary service. *Sacrifice* is the word that these inquirers most frequently use. I have always had three responses to those reactions and the questions that usually accompany them:

The first is that, even if a mission could be regarded as a sacrifice, what I did was nothing compared to what my great-grandfathers and great-great-grandfathers did. The history of the Church is full of heartrending accounts of men who were sent on short notice to preach the gospel, often with few financial resources. They had to leave behind wives and families to support themselves, and they themselves often had no assurance of where the next meal would come from or where they would sleep any given night. And many times, there were no meals and no beds. Today, missionary efforts are much more organized, and missionaries arrange for financial support before they leave. If they are unable

67

to make their own arrangements, the Church will make them.

My second reaction to the suggestion of "sacrifice" is simply that I have never looked at it that way. For me a mission was something I had wanted to do since I was a child. My call to serve as a missionary in Mexico came when I was twenty years old. At the time, it represented *the* climax of my life, and the experience was everything I had hoped for. The most important thing was that it solidified my conviction of the Restoration. While I was a missionary, I truly came to grips with Moroni's promise, "He will manifest the truth of it unto you, by the power of the Holy Ghost" (Moroni 10:4; see also chapter two in this book), because I put it to the test for myself. My greatest satisfaction came in seeing conscientious people develop their own testimonies of the Restoration and change their lives according to their newly developed convictions.

Third, even if those spiritual benefits were left out, the social development and maturity that I experienced in learning to deal with people would have made the thirty-month effort worthwhile. In my particular case, there was an added benefit: acquiring a working knowledge of another culture and another language.

In short, my net assessment of the two-and-one-half years I spent as a missionary in Mexico (foreign-language missions were longer in those days) is a huge plus. I cannot imagine anything else that I could have done during those thirty months that would have given me such long-range benefits. That is, of course, entirely in addition to the benefit of my mission to the people I taught and who accepted the gospel.

My guess is that these feelings are shared by most returned missionaries. I feel certain that all but a very small percentage regard their missions as positive experiences, something they would clearly do again if they had a choice. This certainty is based on all the people I have known or met who served missions. Every one of them has felt that their mission experience was good.

Looking at Mormon missionary life just on its surface, one may be surprised that its participants haven't been more dissatisfied. The young men and women are usually between nineteen and twenty-three — prime ages from both an educational and a social standpoint. The fact that missionaries are not allowed to date only begins to tell the story. The missionary's work day starts very early (usually 6 A.M.) and continues after dinner. The dominant activities consist of proselyting: going door-to-door, contacting people in public, returning to visit previously contacted families, and teaching lessons. During the period of his or her service, the average missionary will also be assigned to ten or so different companions, none of whom he or she chooses. The companions, because they proselyte as pairs, are together almost constantly. There is no comparable social relationship anywhere else in the world. One would think frustration, tension, and pride would be aggravated under such circumstances. (Actually, for all the aggravations, missionary companionships often result in lasting friendships.) How, then, can anyone regard the Mormon missionary experience as tolerable, much less one of life's most memorable and valuable experiences?

I think I know the answers to those questions, but I am

not sure how persuasive they will be to the reader. First, in many contexts, hard work brings feelings of satisfaction. In this respect, missionary work is no exception. Second, the missionaries really believe in what they are doing, and as they begin to see some successes, any frustration becomes inconsequential by comparison. Third, the missionary experience is the only time in their lives that they will be called upon to devote themselves to only one thing. No demands of dating, school, family problems, finances, or employment compete for their time and attention. Most important of all, the single activity in which they are engaged is service to other people, and there is nothing that brings greater happiness. In fact, what they are doing is more beneficial and valuable than anything else they may do in their lifetimes. The Savior put it succinctly when he said that "whosoever will save his life shall lose it: and whosoever will lose his life for my sake shall find it." (Matthew 16:25.)

The two groups most obviously affected by the missionaries' efforts are the men and women themselves and the people they teach. But after having gone through the experience of being a missionary parent, I am convinced that another important recipient group consists of the members of the missionaries' families, who benefit from their experiences vicariously through letters. The parents probably feel the effect most keenly, but brothers and sisters also experience a desire for their siblings' success and a sense of pride and sharing at their siblings' accomplishments in the face of challenges. This experience brings families closer, mostly in a religious sense, but partly out of appreciation for their absent members and a need they feel for unity in supporting those missionaries.

I have talked about my own very unscientific research concerning missionaries' reactions to their mission experiences. Let me suggest that you conduct an equally unscientific experiment yourself. You may know a few Mormons, including some returned missionaries. Ask them whether they would serve a mission again if they had that part of their lives to relive, and watch their faces light up.

CHAPTER 8

THE CHURCH: ORGANIZATION, GOVERNMENT, AND DIVINE AUTHORITY

The "restitution of all things" (Acts 3:21) included a restoration of the basic organization that Jesus established during his time on earth. Some modifications have been made as growth has occurred, but these changes have transpired within the same overall structure established two thousand years ago: apostles, prophets, bishops, priests, teachers, deacons, and others. It is not a structure that human intellect devised; it is the product of Jesus Christ himself, revealed to the apostles and prophets of his time and our time.

The Church of Jesus Christ of Latter-day Saints is organized at three basic levels: (1) the general church, whose officers have worldwide jurisdiction and responsibility; (2) intermediate units, called areas and regions; and (3) the basic congregational units of stakes and wards. A stake has authority over several wards (from four to eight). A ward, which is the basic congregational unit, usually consists of between two and six hundred members. (Stakes derive their name from the stakes of a tent, a metaphor used in Isaiah 54:2 for Zion.) The second level of regions and areas has been incorporated in recent years to accommodate Church growth and facilitate administration.

The dominant characteristic of almost all Church service is that nonprofessionals donate it. There is no such thing as a professional Mormon cleric who has trained for the ministry and then gone into it because he chose to do so. All ecclesiastical positions in the LDS Church, at all levels, are callings, and the calling comes to the individual, through inspiration, from someone else who has the authority and responsibility to make the calling. The people who make the selections consider the possibilities and pray about who should be called to the position. Inspiration also determines when people are to be released and when others should be called.

As a consequence, the tens of thousands of positions, which include responsibilities for attending to the needs of the poor, comforting the widows, administering to the sick, conducting funerals, teaching the gospel, handling administrative and clerical details, serving members, conducting meetings, and counseling families are performed in the Mormon Church not by divinity school graduates, but by men and women age twelve and up who work at regular jobs for a living, who care for their families and homes, or who go to school. Even the ministers of local congregations and larger units, like bishops, stake presidents, and regional representatives, are unpaid ministers. The organization of the Church is truly a lay organization.

This does not mean, however, that trained professionals

have no place in the Church. In cases where members work in administrative or teaching positions that replace secular jobs, those persons receive wages. For example, a well-developed administrative corps of paid staff employees handle the details of welfare, genealogy, missionary work, chapel construction, supply of manuals and other materials, the direction of the Church's educational system, and many other programs for the entire Church. Even locally, persons are hired to do such things as maintain the buildings and lands and administer some parts of the welfare and genealogy programs. There are several thousand such paid jobs at Church headquarters and in the Church educational system (which provides religion classes for college and high school students).

Sermons too are given by local members. The sacrament meetings (Sunday worship services) usually consist of one or two youth speakers who present three- to five-minute sermonettes, and one or two adult speakers, who deliver ten- to fifteen-minute talks. The sermons typically discuss scriptures, doctrine, and principles for living. They cover basically the same range of subjects that other congregations hear from their ministers, priests, or rabbis at Sunday or Saturday worship services. Most active members of the Church — men, women, boys, and girls — have a turn to speak one or more times a year.

How can a church be run efficiently like this? How can it afford to entrust not only the organization, management, and policy making to amateurs, but also the expounding of doctrinal principles? I have two answers to these questions. The first is pragmatic: the system works. The Church has been run this way since its organization in 1830. And quite well. The second is that the fundamental gospel principles of governance, cooperation, participation, and direction by the Spirit are plain and simple. They are principles that can be understood without the benefit of specific, college-level training, by the young and the old. They can be understood and taught today by physicians, carpenters, and computer scientists because they are the same principles that were understood and taught by physicians, carpenters, and fishermen two thousand years ago.

The Church is governed through the authority of God's priesthood, which was restored 160 years ago. The priesthood is the authority and power to act in the name of God. That includes the authority and power to direct when something should occur, under what circumstances it should take place, and who should do it. That authority in its entirety is vested in the President of the Church, who holds all the keys of the priesthood. Very simply, the keys are the power of presidency, the right to preside over and direct any given Church unit.

The keys of an individual ward are vested in the bishop of that ward. He is the one who makes the determination, for example, that baptisms and other ordinances are to be performed and that persons are to be called to positions within the ward. In the case of organizational heads, a president receives the authority and responsibility necessary to direct that organization. Because the bishop holds all the keys within his ward, he can confer specific authority to other individuals according to their responsibilities (he does not give up authority, but rather shares it with others).

The keys a bishop holds are also spiritual in nature. The bishop is entitled to divine inspiration and insight in counseling and assisting members in his ward who need help. At his discretion, he may refer the member to professionals (the Church has a Social Services department to assist members and bishops) for additional help in dealing with specialized problems. In such instances, inspiration may direct that the best way the bishop can deal with a psychiatric or marriage problem is to secure the services of a trained counselor. The priesthood keys of the bishop enable him to carry out all his responsiblities as administrator and spiritual leader of the ward, as well as authorize others to act administratively and spiritually in the myriad duties necessary to the functioning of a ward.

And from whom does the bishop receive his keys? From his presiding officer, the stake president, who holds all the priesthood keys for the stake. The stake president is therefore empowered to confer on any bishop within his stake the keys that pertain to a particular ward. The stake president in turn receives his keys from one of the general officers over the entire church, who acts on behalf of and under the direction of the President of the Church. (These general officers are called General Authorities by members of the Church.)

Crucial to understanding not only the workings of the Mormon Church, but also its doctrine is the fact that all keys of the priesthood are vested in one man, the prophet and President of the Church. Thirteen men have held the office of President since the Church was organized in 1830. So long as the man lives who holds that office, he is the prophet, seer, and revelator for the Church, in whom all keys are vested. Because he holds all the keys, he can call or release any other officer in any position throughout the Church. That also means that when the Lord speaks for purposes of revealing his will to the body of Latter-day Saints, he does so through the prophet.

In addition to his role as President of the Church, the prophet is also the president of one of the three governing quorums of the Church, the Quorum of the First Presidency, which consists of the President and two counselors chosen by him. When the President dies, the Quorum of the First Presidency is dissolved, and the right to exercise the keys of the priesthood devolves upon the Quorum of the Twelve Apostles, which ranks next in authority to the First Presidency but also holds all the keys as a group. A short time thereafter, the senior member of that quorum is ordained President of the Church by the next most senior member of the Quorum, which activates the keys on an individual basis. The new President then selects two counselors, and a new Quorum of the First Presidency is organized.

These two quorums, the Quorum of the First Presidency and the Quorum of the Twelve Apostles, are the Church's main policy-making bodies. The implementation of their policies is shared among these two and the Quorums of the Seventy. The Seventy, like the First Presidency and the Twelve, are General Authorities, and once called to that position, they devote full time to it. As the name implies, their quorum can be composed of as many as seventy men, and like the other two quorums, it traces its origins directly to the Savior's original church. (See Luke 10:1.) The first responsibility of the Seventy in Jesus' time was missionary work, and missionary work remains an important responsibility of the Seventy today. Unlike the First Presidency and the Twelve, the Seventy can be organized into more than one quorum as the Church grows and the need arises. At the present, there are two such quorums. (See D&C 107:6–39 for further explanation of priesthood authority, bishops, and the three governing quorums.)

The final group of General Authorities is the Presiding Bishopric. The Presiding Bishop, together with two counselors he selects, has principal responsibility for the Church's physical affairs. This includes responsibility for facilities, tithes, welfare, and membership records.

A calling as General Authority differs from a stake or ward calling in one important respect: It is a full-time responsibility. General Authorities leave their employment once they have been called. Like all others in the Mormon lay ministry, their professional training and background are in some other field, but unlike their ward and stake counterparts, their general Church calling becomes a full-time job. Apostles serve for life, while members of the First Quorum of Seventy serve until age seventy, health permitting, when they are then granted emeritus status. Members of the Second Quorum of Seventy usually serve five years.

A prominent feature of service within a ward or stake or at the regional level is the nonpermanence of the position. In the typical ward, there are over a hundred separate responsibilities. This means that during the course of his or her life, a member may hold dozens of different Church positions. Besides giving the member a variety and depth of experience, this aspect of service helps prevent the formation of a hierarchy of various positions.

For example, about thirteen years ago, I was called to serve as a stake president. After I was released, I was called to be a Sunday School teacher for a class of fourteen-year-olds. Several years later, another person then serving as stake president called me to be a bishop, just as I had earlier called bishops. At the time I was a bishop, one of the members of the stake presidency who presided over me was a man who had served as my counselor when I was a stake president. That means that my former counselor later functioned as my ecclesiastical supervisor. My calling at the time of this book's publication is a Sunday School teacher for sixteen-year-olds.

This obviously does not work like the military, or like a corporation, or like other churches' clergy. No hierarchy exists through which one, by his or her diligence and demonstrated ability, ascends step by step. At different times in one's life, the Lord will call the member to serve in the different capacities he needs the person to serve in at that time. Of course, some positions exercise directional authority over other positions, but the object or pattern is not to move "up" but to view all positions as important and work where the Lord wishes.

The participatory nature of Church work and the frequent changing of positions mean that the responsibility for the success of the ward rests with every member, not just with the bishop and other key ward leaders. As a consequence, if I conclude that things are going better in some other ward, I do not start attending another ward; I do what

I can to make things better where I am. Since wards are organized along geographic boundaries, members do not switch congregations unless they move. If my bishop or Relief Society president or Sunday School teacher turns out to be not as good as someone else on the other side of town, I do not switch wards. I try to be tolerant and loving, working to improve things through my responsibilities. The fact that I could someday be in that person's place helps put things in perspective.

How large an impact does one's Church calling have on one's life? The general answer to those questions is, a lot. The more specific answer is that the precise amount depends mainly on one's calling at the moment, and how efficient he or she is.

Any active member of the Church who attends worship services and has any kind of Church calling will spend an average of five to ten hours a week on Church activities (three hours in Sunday meetings; one or more hours a week preparing and performing one's calling and attending several monthly meetings related to the calling; and some hours each month for temple attendance, stake meetings, and home teaching or visiting teaching assignments). At the other end of the spectrum, a bishop, stake president, or president of a ward or stake Relief Society or youth program can average twenty to twenty-five hours a week (and more when several crises manage to come at the same time).

These are, to be sure, major demands, but the people called to Church positions are usually convinced of the truth of the Restoration. Performance of these callings brings a satisfaction that is profound and enduring and that cannot

81

be experienced in other ways. This is especially true of the more time-consuming callings. People feel good about these callings for the same reasons that devoted missionaries feel good about their missions.

The demands on time occasionally create some stress for the individual and in the family. Surprisingly, not all Mormons squarely face or even acknowledge this problem. The amount of time and involvement in Church responsibilities can be considerable, and thus Latter-day Saint parents and Church leaders need to be constantly aware of the problem. One precaution observed in almost all wards today is that both parents are not usually given time-consuming Church callings at the same time. In addition, I think that the children of parents who have demanding Church jobs receive as many benefits from a home dedicated to the Lord's work as drawbacks stemming from fewer hours at home.

"Well, all right," the reader may be thinking, "I can understand that your doctrine and organization are different, and your Church is run by people from all walks of life. But why does that mean you have to be so inhospitable, so standoffish to other churches? Won't you agree that other churches do a lot of good and teach a lot of truth? If so, why don't you join forces with them like other, morally minded good citizens?"

Actually, we admire, support, and are grateful for the work done by other churches. Their teachings and practices contain much truth, and we make a real effort locally and worldwide to be cooperative in achieving common objectives with other churches. We are active in both national and international religious associations and attempt, where possible, to coordinate our philanthropic efforts with those of other churches so as to enhance their effectiveness as well as ours.

Ecumenism itself, however, in its core sense would require a lowest-common-denominator doctrinal reduction that would take the heart out of Mormonism. In the doctrinal sense, it would require denial of the very things that make us what we are. This is not just another church. Joseph Smith was not another Martin Luther. The Book of Mormon is not just a set of good ideas that came from the pen of an intelligent, creative writer. Performance of the saving ordinances requires direct authority from God himself. Being an orderly God, he does not spread it around indiscriminately among a variety of organizations that teach a variety of doctrines. He vests that authority, just as he always has from Adam's day on, in the single organization that was founded by him and teaches his doctrines.

Complete ecumenism would require either that The Church of Jesus Christ of Latter-day Saints deny its divine authority or that others in the ecumenical movement accept it, neither of which is possible. This does not prevent, however, all Christians from cooperating as fully as they can consistent with their principles and respecting each other in those areas where agreement is not possible.

CHAPTER 9

ORDINANCES FOR THE DEAD:
GENEALOGICAL AND TEMPLE WORK

What is a Mormon temple? Is it a congregational meeting house, open to the public, or does it have a more specific purpose? And why are so many Mormons such avid genealogists? Does historical research into one's ancestors have some religious significance? And if it does, what would it be?

The answers to those questions cover one of the most important areas of Latter-day Saint belief and practice — that is, providing for the exaltation of our ancestors who died without the opportunity of hearing and accepting the gospel, and performing on their behalf the ordinances of salvation, which include baptism, confirmation, temple marriage, and others.

Leaders of the Mormon Church have stated frequently that the threefold mission of the Church is to perfect the members, preach the gospel to all the world, and redeem the dead. This mission focuses on making the gospel, its message, and its benefits available to three groups of people:

living Church members, living nonmembers, and our ancestors.

To some, the third purpose — redeem the dead — seems a bit far-fetched, even a bit eerie. Who ever heard of converting dead people? Or baptizing them? The simple reason that many don't associate vicarious work for the dead with religious ministries is that this is one of the principles of the original Church lost from the earth for many centuries and then restored. The fifteenth chapter of 1 Corinthians contains Paul's classic rebuttal of the proposition espoused by the Sadducees and others that there is no resurrection. Among the arguments that Paul advanced to prove the resurrection was that if there were no resurrection, and therefore no afterlife, there would be no point in doing baptisms for the dead. Paul's specific words were "Else what shall they do which are baptized for the dead, if the dead rise not at all? why are they then baptized for the dead?" (1 Corinthinans 15:29.)

Paul was using a well-recognized and reliable advocate's device. He was relying on a well-established fact — one that would be commonly accepted and recognized — as a basis for supporting another proposition that was not so well-established. In his case, the established fact was baptisms for the dead, and he used this fact to make his point. There would be little purpose in performing baptisms for the dead if there were no resurrection.

We realize from this scripture that in ancient times baptism for the dead was a well-recognized practice. Note that whereas resurrection/no resurrection was something that neither Paul nor the Sadducees could scientifically prove, the practice of baptisms for the dead was not open to debate. It was actually happening. The only question, Paul argued, was whether it was a useless act.

Similarly, the scriptures provide a solid foundation for missionary work among deceased people—giving them the opportunity they may or may not have had in this life to accept or reject the Gospel. The First Epistle of Peter, for example, reports that the Savior, during the interim between his death and resurrection, preached to the souls of those who had slumbered, who in the days of Noah had been disobedient. (See 1 Peter 3:18–20.)

The basic notion of proselyting and performing ordinances for deceased people may at first strike some as not being very logical, notwithstanding the scriptures showing that the Savior and his apostles actually did it. On analysis, however, it makes perfectly good sense. Once one understands the basic principles of the Restoration, discussed in preceding chapters, one should understand that including our ancestors in the proselyting effort is not only consistent, but requisite.

The starting point for the analysis is the existence of one true church founded upon apostles and prophets and vested with the authority to carry out God's work on earth. The Savior established this church in ancient times, and the foundation of apostles and prophets was described by Paul as essential until all come to a unity of the faith. (See Ephesians 2:19–20.) It is that same Church with the same organization and the same priesthood authority that has once again been brought back to earth, in keeping with what Peter called "the restitution of all things." (Acts 3:21.)

The next step in the analysis is the need for ordinances, which can be performed only by persons having authority to perform them. The pivotal ordinance, as discussed in chapter four, is baptism, an ordinance without which there can be no exaltation. Both the Savior and his apostles made that very clear. The scriptures also clarify that baptism is exclusively an earthly ordinance. (See John 3:3–5; D&C 20:37.) In short, baptism is essential — it must be performed by one having authority, and it must be performed on this earth.

It would be manifestly unfair to relegate the millions of people who have lived on this earth and never had the opportunity to hear the gospel to be precluded from the blessings of exaltation. This problem — what happens to those who never heard the gospel? — is, in fact, a question that has baffled Christian denominations for centuries. The answers men have devised are varied, and few find any of them satisfactory. Given the requirements for salvation, everyone deserves a chance, and everyone must have that chance. And that is why we do genealogical and temple work, or family history work, as members call this area of service.

Logistically, to be sure, the task is an awesome one, but the effort that the Church has put forth has been equally impressive. In all parts of the world, the Church has spent decades of time and many millions of dollars in gathering genealogical records. There have been substantial incidental benefits from this effort to persons and organizations other than the Church. In most countries, the microfilm documents were taken from records of other churches, each of which was given a copy of the microfilm, which will be much easier to preserve in the future than the original records. Other benefits to genealogists and historians are obvious, and the Church makes its family history libraries freely accessible to all users.

But the principal purpose, and the principal use for these records is to identify our kindred dead (as we like to call them) so that, as in the days of the Apostle Paul, the saving ordinances can be performed on their behalf.

Does this mean that in our view, the ordinances will all be effective, regardless of the views of the individuals for whom the work is done? The answer is no. As is the case with the living, the dead also must have an opportunity to hear the gospel and to accept and reject it. This is accomplished in an intermediate stage between death and the resurrection described by the Prophet Alma in the Book of Mormon as the "state of the soul." (Alma 40:11–14.) This is generally referred to as the "spirit world." Like the world in which we now live, the spirit world is a place outside the presence of our Heavenly Father and outside our memory of the premortal life so that agency and the need to choose still prevail. We believe that missionary work continues all the time in that spirit world, just as the Savior preached to those who had been rebellious in the time of Noah. Some of our ancestors will respond favorably to those proselyting efforts, and some will not. For those who do not accept it, the vicarious ordinances will simply have no effect. For those who do, the ordinances will be fully acceptable to the Lord, just as Paul reminded the Corinthians. (See 1 Corinthians 15:29.)

Some obvious logistical problems are involved. One results from the sheer numbers of people involved. The work must ultimately be done for billions of people, and the complete package of ordinance work done in the temple for any given individual presently takes about three hours. Nevertheless, the task is brought into a more manageable perspective by two things. First, each individual and each family concentrate on their own immediate ancestors. A great many extended families have organized and combined efforts in this respect so as to avoid duplication. Second, a period of a thousand years called the Millennium will follow the second coming of the Savior, during which the forces of evil will be stayed, and that will be a great period for catching up on the backlog.

Concentrating our individual and family efforts on our immediate ancestors is more than just a matter of administrative efficiency. It also makes the research more interesting and personalizes the effort. Most people really want to know about their ancestors. Who was my great-grandfather? Who was my great-great-grandmother? What kind of people were they? Where did they live, what did they do, and in what respects were their lives different from mine? Can I see in them any of the characteristics that still prevail in my generation of the family? Are there things I can learn from their lives that will be helpful to me?

The Church encourages family history research that reaches beyond the bare identification of statistical data such as birth, marriage, and death. Tens of thousands of genealogical researchers have become better acquainted with their ancestors and developed a closer kinship with them through searching out their genealogical records. Many family organizations have published books, largely for distribution within the family, concerning their ancestors. My experience with respect to several branches of my own family and with respect to others I have observed is that these family histories are intensely interesting and valuable: we like to know from what kind of stock we came. Studying our ancestors makes our own lives more full and more interesting. And I am sure that most of us harbor the hope that some of our descendants will have an interest in us and what we did.

For Mormon genealogists, however, there is an added dimension: the knowledge that they are not only learning more about their ancestors, but are also providing the means for their eternal salvation, including the opportunity to be united as one family with the researcher during the eternities.

Commensurate with its importance, the restoration of the keys of genealogical and temple work occurred quite early. That restoration was accomplished by Elijah the prophet (the same one who confounded the priests of Baal), and it occurred on April 3, 1836, in the Kirtland Temple. (See D&C 110:13–16.) Over two millennia prior to the time that this restoration occurred, the prophet Malachi described both the fact of the restoration of genealogical and temple work and the effect that these would have on the feelings of descendants for their ancestors and ancestors for the descendants. Malachi said: "Behold, I will send you Elijah the prophet before the coming of the great and dreadful day of the Lord: and he shall turn the heart of the fathers to the children, and the heart of the children to the fathers, lest I come and smite the earth with a curse." (Malachi 4: 5–6.)

That is exactly what has happened. The Lord sent Elijah the prophet to Joseph Smith in the Kirtland Temple, and he bestowed on Joseph the keys of genealogical and temple work. And as countless members of the Church who have been active in this effort can testify, the result has been that the hearts of the children have been turned to their fathers. I assume that the other part is also true, that the hearts of the fathers have been turned to the children. We will be able to check that with them when we see our ancestors face to face after we pass away, and we will learn of their reactions to what we have been doing for them.

This matter of turning the hearts of the children to the fathers and vice versa is not, I think, limited to those who gather data for the necessary saving ordinances. I suspect that people who do genealogical research as a hobby also develop a closeness to their ancestors that can accurately be described as a turning of the hearts of the children to the fathers. In any event, there is no doubt that this happens to Church members researching their ancestors. Great-great-grandparents, long-deceased aunts and uncles come alive. They become real to us. Though we have never met them, we feel a kinship with them and an increased appreciation for their sacrifices and ideals and loyalties. This kinship is enhanced by the knowledge that we are providing them the opportunity to accept those ordinances, without which the Savior said that "he cannot enter into the kingdom of God." (John 3:5.)

The second step in making the gospel available to our ancestors consists of the performance of vicarious ordinances. These are performed in the temples, of which there were forty-four in operation and six either under construction or in planning stages by the end of 1992, located throughout the world. The word *temple* for Latter-day Saints does not mean the meetinghouse where weekly and other meetings open to the public are held. The temple is more limited in its purpose. It is the place where four ordinances for the living and all of the necessary ordinances for the dead are performed. The four ordinances for the living are eternal marriage, discussed in chapter three, washings and anointings (also called the initiatory ordinances), and the endowment.

Washing and anointing are similar, one using water and the other using olive oil. Men administer the ordinance to men, and women administer them to women. Like the washing and anointing of ancient priests of Israel to stand as representatives of the Lord, the washing and anointing are symbolic acts of purification and consecration.

The heart of the endowment is a series of covenants or promises that the individual makes to Heavenly Father, with certain blessings coming to that individual if those covenants are kept. (See D&C 130:20–21; 132:6–7.) These covenants are set in a dramatic narrative that teaches about the Creation and the purpose of earthly life. It takes about two hours to complete.

In the cases of ordinances for the living, each person participates in the ordinance once for him- or herself. Subsequent trips to the temple — which for active Church members occur several times a year—are for the purpose of performing the four ordinances and the other saving ordinances (baptism, confirmation, and ordination to the priesthood) vicariously on behalf of an ancestor or another specifically identified person. While each person has a primary responsibility to search out the names and do the work for his or her own ancestors, there is no requirement that vicarious ordinances be performed only by relatives. Thus, in God's plan of salvation, we can truly say that all will have a chance to hear of and accept Jesus Christ and his gospel, and all will have a chance to believe, obey his commandments, and receive the ordinances he has given for salvation.

CHAPTER 10

THE EXERCISE OF PRIESTHOOD —
AUTHORITY AND
AUTHORITARIANISM

One of the great concerns of religion and religious bodies
is authority. How much authority should a church excercise
over its adherents? The greater the control, the more authoritarian the church. In this light, many ask, Is the Mormon
Church authoritarian toward its members in general and
toward women in particular?

In at least one sense, the answer to the question has to
be yes. There can be little doubt that the church run by the
Savior during his three-year mission on earth was authoritarian in the sense that people did what he said because
they recognized him as one having authority. Similarly, a
modern church led by apostles and prophets called of God
and chosen by him for the purpose of administering his
kingdom on earth can hardly be on a par with organizations
like a driver's license bureau with its administrators and
managers or the U.S. Congress with its congressmen.

In matters of doctrine, what the prophet, under Jesus

Christ's leadership, declares is definitive and inarguable. For example, when President Spencer W. Kimball announced on June 8, 1978, that the priesthood was to be available to all worthy male members (thus repealing the exclusion of blacks), there was no debate. The Prophet had spoken on a matter that was clearly one of doctrine, and there the matter began and ended. It is the kind of thing that must make presidents and prime ministers envious. But anything else would be inconsistent with the fact of the Restoration.

Most important day-to-day issues in the Church, however, do not involve matters of doctrine — at least not so clearly as did the revelation on blacks and the priesthood. What roles do discussion and disagreement play in these areas?

With respect to Church administration and government, both ends of the spectrum are represented. Functionally, the Mormon Church is dynamic. It constantly devises new ways to carry out its basic objectives. Most of these come from the general Church leaders, and the acceptance rate by the people who implement them is very high. Some may say, "I wonder whether this is really a very good idea," but the dominant attitude is, "The leaders want us to try this, and we will give it our best."

Providing criticism and feedback concerning the success of the program as it develops through actual experiences is an entirely different matter. On these matters, most local Church leaders speak their minds openly and regularly, and regular semiannual stake conferences and other special meetings provide ample opportunity to do so.

What about matters of secular government and public policy? Are the Church's stands in these matters also binding on the Church members? These issues do not come up very often, because the Church does not often take official positions on other than moral issues. During my adult lifetime, I remember three such issues. One was repeal of Section 14 b of the National Labor Relations Act, which establishes federal policy with respect to right-to-work laws as a national matter. The second was the Equal Rights Amendment, and the third, the debate over the MX missile.

Regardless of how frequent or infrequent these pronouncements by Church leaders on issues of government and public policy, the fact is they do occur from time to time. What is their effect? How much weight do Mormons give them?

On the one hand, most Mormons evidently support the Church's stance on issues when it takes one. On the other hand, the pronouncements probably do not receive the same universal, unqualified support enjoyed by the Standard Works. While reactions vary all the way from "The Church should stay out of politics" to "The General Authorities have spoken, and that's good enough for me," probably the predominant reaction is along these lines: "This is the General Authorities' position, and I want to support it if I possibly can. One of their responsibilities is deciding when they should take positions on issues of this kind." Many members will then make the issues a matter of prayer and study. In short, there is a general attitude of deference toward Church leaders' views.

I do not view this as at all inconsistent with the existence of a living prophet. None of the three statements on public policy discussed above was preceded by the words "Thus saith the Lord," nor was there any other indication that the message came by way of revelation. If any were ever so prefaced, it would fit in an entirely different category: it would qualify for, and I am confident would receive, unqualified and virtually universal deference by faithful members of the Church.

Now that I have stated that my Church, which I like very much, is in a sense entitled to a label ("authoritarian"), which I dislike very much, let me offer a couple of other perspectives, in addition to the one discussed at the outset: that it is authoritative in the same way that the Savior's original church was authoritative; that it is authoritative because it has the authority.

The first perspective begins by asking the question, "What is authoritarianism, and why is it that people generally dislike it?" I said a moment ago that it is one of my least favorite adjectives. Why is that? It is because authoritarianism connotes the imposition by a larger or otherwise stronger entity of its own views upon a person and against that person's will. In other words, many people equate authoritarian with domineering. To truly be an authoritarian, one should not be an official in a voluntary organization. The best place for true authoritarians is probably in government — specifically, a government from which people's opportunity to resign or withdraw because of their displeasure at its antics is usually more theoretical than real. To whatever extent authority is exercised in the Mormon Church to influence people's behavior, it is done by consensus. And this makes it unauthoritarian.

Second, using priesthood authority in any sort of a subjugating fashion is directly contrary to modern scripture. One of the most moving passages of scripture in all of the Standard Works is in the 121st section of the Doctrine and Covenants, which reads in part: "There are many called, but few are chosen. And why are they not chosen? Because their hearts are set so much upon the things of this world, and aspire to the honors of men, that they do not learn this one lesson—that the rights of the priesthood are inseparably connected with the powers of heaven, and that the powers of heaven cannot be controlled nor handled only upon the principles of righteousness. . . .

"No power or influence can or ought to be maintained by virtue of the priesthood, only by persuasion, by long-suffering, by gentleness and meekness, and by love un-feigned; by kindness, and pure knowledge, which shall greatly enlarge the soul without hypocrisy, and without guile." (Verses 34–42.)

Third, the true authoritarian does not spread power broadly; he or she attempts to keep it confined to as small a group as possible. In The Church of Jesus Christ of Latter-day Saints, priesthood authority is not only shared with every male in the world twelve years of age or older who will accept it and try to live righteously, but a large portion of the Church's resources is also devoted to persuading more people to accept this authority. It is no answer to say that the real authority is kept vested in two groups, one of which consists of three and the other of twelve men located in Salt Lake City. For explained in chapter seven, the authority of the President of the Church is shared throughout the Church.

Some protest that the priesthood is given to every worthy

male over twelve years of age. What about females? Doesn't this distinction discriminate against women? Many also point to the fact that the Church opposed the Equal Rights Amendment. Are these things generally indicative of an attitude that women are, in the Church's view, the view of its men, and perhaps even in the view of many of its women, some kind of second-class citizens?

As in the case of any organization, there are, sadly, individual priesthood holders whose attitudes toward women stem from the most elementary gender-based biases. Whatever their numbers — I hope they are small, and I think they are, though in some instances quite visible — I hope that those numbers will diminish in time. And I think they will at about the same rate that our society itself becomes more sophisticated about the subtleties of sex discrimination. One of the real tragedies of sex discrimination is that those afflicted with the malady are seldom aware of its causes, symptoms, or even its existence.

Individual instances of insensitivity and malpractice cannot change the fact that the Church itself condemns discrimination in any form, and it has so instructed its leaders throughout the world that this is Church policy. In a statement concerning the Equal Rights Amendment, the First Presidency said: "In Utah, where our Church is headquartered, women received the right to vote in 1870, fifty years before the Nineteenth Amendment to the Constitution granted the right nationally.

"There have been injustices to women before the law and in society generally. These we deplore." (Statement of the First Presidency on the Equal Rights Amendment, 22

October 1976, quoted in "The Church and the Proposed Equal Rights Amendment: A Moral Issue," *Ensign,* February 1980, page 21.)

More specifically, those who argue that the Church's attitude toward women is less than what it should be usually premise their contentions on the facts that women do not hold the priesthood and that the Church opposed the Equal Rights Amendment. I will deal with each of these issues briefly.

The question of the persons to whom the priesthood is given is a scriptural one. At one time its holders were limited to the male adult members of a single tribe, the Levites. (See Numbers 8:13–22; Deuteronomy 18:1–2.) The apostolic church extended it to male adult members of the House of Israel, and today all worthy male members of the requisite age are eligible. To my knowledge, women as a group have never been eligible. Of course, some say that they would expect that from a patriarchal, male-dominated society. However, for reasons the Lord has not clearly identified, he established the priesthood lines of authority himself.

Will the priesthood ever be extended to women in the future? The answer to that question would require speculation of the grandest sort, which neither I nor any other mortal person would be able to engage in profitably. The only relevant point is that public debate will not decide who is to be given the priesthood. That decision belongs to the same being as it has for the past six millennia—the Lord himself, speaking through his prophet. The important point is that the present circumstance, as it has in the past, does not result from any surge of discriminatory attitudes toward women. Rather, it derives from the content of revelations.

While the priesthood itself is held only by men, its blessings and other effects are shared by all. As discussed in chapter seven, authority is distributed to members according to their callings. The president in a Primary presidency, for instance, is set apart to her calling and given the authority and responsibility to govern that organization. Church members are accustomed to a high level of participation in all aspects of their church unit and its activities, and women participate in a very real sense as much as men.

As for the family, an understanding of the family as an eternal unit gives an extra dimension to the concept of the mother and father as equal sharing partners within that family unit. The man may hold the priesthood, but both are equally responsible for teaching their children, supporting each other, and making decisions together. Most important, neither may enjoy eternal life without the other.

The Church's opposition to the Equal Rights Amendment has been widely misunderstood. Unfortunately, the leaders of the effort to pass that amendment effectively created the impression that the world was divided into two groups of people: those who favored enactment of the Equal Rights Amendment, and those who favored discrimination against women. In fact, I concluded during the course of debates and discussions with some of those leaders that many truly held that dichotomous belief. But such a view is just plain wrong. There were good, sound reasons for opposing the Equal Rights Amendment wholly aside from one's views about how society ought to treat women. Several years ago I felt strongly enough to set those reasons forth in a book, *A Lawyer Looks at the Equal Rights Amendment* (Provo:

Brigham Young University Press, 1980). I explore those reasons in detail there.

I consider one of the most important reasons to be the fact that both Congress and the state legislatures already have the constitutional authority they need to pass whatever antidiscrimination statutes they believe to be in the interests of their constituents. They have passed and continue to pass such laws; we experience the good and bad effects of those laws, keep most of them and repeal some; and the system seems to be working quite well. To be sure, sex discrimination is still a serious problem. There are also many other serious public policy problems, and we don't solve all of them by constitutional amendments, even if statutes could resolve them. The reason is that a constitutional amendment takes away the public's ability to deal flexibly with a difficult public policy problem — to experiment with one approach, and then, if it doesn't work, to try another. (My earlier book discusses the reasons why the proposed Equal Rights Amendment would have been an example of a restrictive, inflexible amendment.)

The matter essentially comes down to a conscientious effort by Church leaders to deal with a difficult and important problem: the conflicts that come into a woman's life because of the tensions between her efforts to care for her home and children on the one hand, and her efforts to further her own growth and development on the other. Both are particularly important to Mormons — the family, because it is the central and basic unit in the eternal scheme of things, and individual growth, because that is one of life's three great purposes. Accordingly, the tension between the two

103

is no small matter, and the Equal Rights Amendment would not resolve that but would rather heighten it.

These conflicts are not easy issues. In some instances, the woman may not be deriving any real growth from her employment, and in the children's interest, the family can and should make do with the husband's salary. But this description does not fit all cases. While we believe that children greatly benefit from one of the parents being home when they are, that does not necessarily have to be the mother. It can be the father, or the two can work out their schedules so that the responsibilities are shared. I know some couples — in each case both the husband and wife are professionals — who use some variation of that system with varying degrees of success.

Not surprisingly, different leaders of the Church tend to give different emphases to the two values at issue.

One example of statements emphasizing the value of the mother in the home is the following from President N. Eldon Tanner, a counselor in the First Presidency: "I would urge all husbands, fathers, sons, and brothers to show great respect and love and try to be worthy of the women who are our wives, mothers, daughters, sisters, and sweethearts. There is no surer way for a man to show his lack of character, of good breeding, and of quality than for him to show lack of respect for woman or to do anything that would discredit or degrade her. It is unchristianlike, unfair, and displeasing to God for any husband or father to assume the role of dictator and adopt the attitude that he is superior in any way to his wife." ("No Greater Honor: The Woman's Role," in *Woman* [Salt Lake City: Deseret Book Company, 1979], page 11.)

Many General Authorities have also suggested that, while women should involve themselves in community affairs and in the auxiliary organizations of the Church, they should always remember that home and children come first and must not be neglected. Children must be made to feel that mother and father love them and are keenly interested in their welfare and everything they do. This cannot be turned over to someone else.

An example of the emphasis on the value of individual development is this statement from Elder John A. Widtsoe, an apostle of the Church: "The right of woman to develop her native gifts through education has been held before the Church from its organization. Women have, indeed, been urged to train for the various life pursuits of society. The fine arts, music, painting, literature, teaching, business, science, mining, medicine, civil government and law were mentioned by Brigham Young as suitable studies for women. ... President Joseph F. Smith spoke similarly: 'It is very important to the welfare, usefulness, happiness, and comfort of our daughters (in view of certain circumstances) that they learn some branch of industry that could be turned to practical account in the way of making a living, should circumstances require it.' " (John A. Widtsoe, "Evidences and Reconciliations: XLVII—What Is the Place of Woman in the Church?" *The Improvement Era,* March 1942, page 161.)

What is the right accommodation of these two values? Does it vary from family to family and circumstance to circumstance? The Lord has said to take care of our families and to develop in intelligence. The balance is found, in my opinion, through the same methods used to resolve any of the other hundreds of issues we face — through study, prayer, and the exercise of our agency in all good conscience. Such confrontations and resolutions are part of the developmental experience that is one of the three great purposes of this life.

CHAPTER 11

CHURCH INFLUENCE: WHAT ROLE DO INVESTMENTS AND POLITICAL OFFICE-HOLDERS PLAY?

In recent years, several writers have stressed one or both of two related themes. The first is that the Church has acquired a vast financial empire, consisting of properties that are not central to its mission as a church, and the second is that Mormons enjoy a disproportionately high percentage of the influential positions in government, at least during Republican administrations. The implication (or in some cases, more than implication) of the writings is that both of these are improper endeavors for the Church to be involved in and that they somehow pose a threat to the interests of non-Mormons. (See, generally, John Heinerman and Anson Shupe, *The Mormon Corporate Empire* [Boston: Beacon Press, 1988]; and Robert Gottlieb and Peter Wiley, *America's Saints* [San Diego: Harcourt Brace Jovanovich, 1986].) Though these issues only tangentially touch upon what Mormons believe, the themes are important enough to warrant a short discussion.

Let's look at the facts first and then the possible motives. Like most other churches, the LDS Church is reluctant to produce many figures concerning its financial affairs. However, Gordon B. Hinckley, first counselor in the First Presidency, said: "The Church has substantial assets necessary to its program. These assets are primarily in buildings. They are in ward and stake meeting facilities, in schools and seminaries, colleges and institutes. They are in welfare projects. These assets are in mission homes and missionary training centers, temples and family history archives, as well as related activities and facilities all concerned directly with our mission. But it should be recognized that all of these are money-consuming assets and not money-producing assets. They are expensive to build and maintain. They do not produce financial wealth, but they do much to strengthen and build Latter-day Saints.

"We have a few income-producing business properties, but the return from these would keep the Church going only for a very brief time." ("The State of the Church," *Ensign*, May 1991, page 54.)

The affairs of any church whose membership is in the eight-million range are bound to have some complexities, and this includes financial affairs. One simply cannot expect that the financial interests of a church of that size will be limited to paying for and maintaining the places where its members meet. The achievement of those direct religious objectives will almost certainly be less effective if the Church's financial vision is so limited. Moreover, drawing a clear distinction between those investments that serve religious objectives and those that do not is not always easy.

A prime example is the Church's rather extensive holdings of radio and television properties.

As a matter of policy, which is probably influenced by requirements of federal law, the Church's television and radio stations, owned and operated by a separate, wholly owned subsidiary of the Church, Bonneville International Corporation, are not used directly for proselyting purposes. But the Church has a proper interest in not only its direct proselyting, but also its other more indirect efforts to share the message of the Restoration with the world. Church leaders have also stated often the Church's responsibility to improve the intellectual and moral climate within which its total mission is to be accomplished. All of these are affected through the processes of communication.

I have always been amused by the suggestion that the Church has some independent objective to amass wealth. For reasons developed in earlier chapters, the Church to which I belong is not just another church. It is the vehicle through which Jesus Christ has restored his full gospel, including the requisite authority and organization. Everything that the Church does—including the acquisition of financial holdings—is necessarily adjunct to that important, overriding objective.

Very simply, the Church does not enter into its various endeavors for any purpose other than the ultimate one of building the restored kingdom of Jesus Christ. The fact that its leaders take a broad view of the activities that will assist in accomplishing that mission—extending from colleges and universities, to television and radio stations, to welfare service projects, and many others—is evidence of the impor-

109

tance and complexity of the mission, as well as the variety of means that can contribute to its fulfillment. If the accumulation of wealth were even one of the Church's objectives, it certainly would not place the overwhelming majority of its assets in income-consuming rather than income-producing investments.

Finally, even assuming that the Church did have as an independent objective the acquisition of as much worldly wealth as possible, this would seem principally a matter of concern only for Church members. How would anyone else's legitimate interests be adversely affected? Furthermore, if the interests of other people are ever affected by the investment decisions of this or any other church, the Congress of the United States or the legislative body of the nation or the affected locality can pass any protective laws that are needed, so long as they are consistent with constitutional guarantees. The other protection—with a shorter reaction time—comes from the members themselves.

Since shortly after the turn of the century, the Church has been out of debt. The payment of tithes and the careful management of Church finances and resources have created that enviable position. In fact, today the Church will not build any facility until it is paid for, including chapels in foreign countries that are far too expensive for members to afford if they had to pay for the buildings themselves. In addition, it now pays the operating costs of every ward and stake in the world and the maintenance costs of all its facilities. That the Church handles huge amounts of money is obvious because of its tithing, fast offering, and welfare programs. That the Church's income goes into the vast expenses of maintaining and expanding Church programs and properties worldwide should be equally as obvious.

I turn now to the proposition that too many Mormons are serving in government, even though the proposition seems to me to be ludicrous. The argument appears to be limited to, or at least focused upon higher, appointive or elected policy-making positions, primarily in the federal government.

At the outset, I am not sure exactly what number is disproportionately high, or how one would make that determination. On two occasions, 1975–77 and 1981–85, I held a presidential appointment, the first time as Assistant Attorney General in charge of the Civil Division and the second as Solicitor General of the United States. I know that both times, there were other Mormons who served in government with me, some of them in high-ranking, policy-making positions.

But I do not know how to determine what is a "fair share" for any religious group. Certainly in making the determination one would not count an assistant secretary the same as a section chief, or the same as a cabinet officer. And it would be rather difficult, I suppose, to assign weights to different positions and then determine when a particular religious group had exceeded the number of authorized weighted points that one would expect.

Even if one could make such a calculation, and even if it could be determined that from time to time or even all the time, Mormons have had a larger share of these positions than the size of the Church would warrant, the question still remains: Why should anyone possibly be concerned? The

111

majority of citizens, for instance, have become open-minded enough to accept a Catholic president (a big issue of the past, sad to say). Is there enough prejudice left to care about the religious affiliation of any future president? Evidently, there is.

First, let me assure you that no conspiracy exists to put Mormons into high government positions in order to enhance the Church's interests. If there were, I would have known about it, because in the mid-1970s and the early 1980s I would have had to belong to such a supposed effort. A conspiracy between the Church and its governmental officials would not be much of a conspiracy if it did not include the Solicitor General.

Second, one would have to ask what the objectives of such a conspiracy might be and what the possibilities are that such objectives could be achieved, even if the group purportedly achieving them wanted to. The notion that the Mormon Church could take over the government is ridiculous. Moreover, why would it want to? Probably no organization has benefited as much from constitutional government as the Mormon Church. The Church's stake is in the continuance of constitutional government. Its objective is to make the message of the Restoration available to as many people as possible, and then to continue to minister to the needs of those who voluntarily accept it. It is a program which works best under the protection of exactly the kind of government that now exists in the United States.

A more realistic objective would be to influence periodic decisions of government in a way favorable to the Church, much as lobbying groups do. Perhaps the suggestion is that

so long as active Mormons are placed in positions of responsibility, their decisions will automatically favor the interests of their church.

The situation may be different with respect to Congress,
but at least in the Executive Branch even the opportunity
to sacrifice governmental interests for Church interests
rarely occurs. During my confirmation hearings to be the
Solicitor General, one senator was particularly concerned
as to how I would handle situations in which the interests
of my church conflicted with those of the government. I
assured him that my employer was the United States of
America, and it was to that employer that my loyalties would
run. I would therefore attempt to determine the interests
of the United States and pursue those, regardless of the
impact on interests of other groups to which I might belong,
including my church.

I did not have to abandon or twist my membership in
or allegiance to the Church to make such a statement. The
Church urges participation in civil affairs but stresses independence at the same time. Furthermore, the concerns
of the Church deal with moral and spiritual issues, and
though law and government don't often overtly include
those, we all hope that morality is the driving force behind
good government.

During my four years in office, only one instance arose
that posed a possible conflict. The Mormon Church, along
with many other churches and some nonreligious organizations, had filed an *amicus curiae* (friend of the court)
brief urging the United States Supreme Court to grant *certiorari* (agreeing to review on the merits) in a particular

113

case to which the United States was a party. After reviewing the case, I concluded, contrary to the position taken by the Church and others, that the Supreme Court should not review the case on the merits, that justice had been done in the lower courts, and that no need existed for further review. I so informed the Supreme Court, which then denied *certiorari* as I had recommended. If I had felt that the interests of the United States would be served by taking the same position my church took, I would have so argued to the Supreme Court. But I did not so conclude, and therefore urged the Court not to grant review.

With respect to the two issues discussed in this chapter, The Church of Jesus Christ of Latter-day Saints is not very different from other churches. It attempts to use its money and other resources in ways that will, over the long run, further its religious objectives. And like any other church, it likes its members to succeed in those things that they enjoy doing, including those members who serve in government positions. With respect to neither of these, however, is the Church engaged in some clandestine effort to exercise influence that should not be exercised. And if it did have such an objective, it would not work.

WHY AM I A MORMON?

There are practical reasons why I am pleased and proud to be a Mormon. I am proud of my ancestors who, along with other Mormon pioneers, made the long trek across a forbidding and inhospitable wasteland from Illinois to Utah. They sacrificed property, health, and in some cases their lives because of their religious convictions. In the process, they carved a unique and enduring niche in our nation's history and cultural traditions.

On a more personal level, my life is happier and fuller because of my beliefs and my Church membership. Those beliefs positively influence my values and my ethical and moral standards, as well as the values and standards of my family.

However, the principal reason I am glad to be a Mormon is not because of my religion's good and practical effects on my life. As I have stated throughout this book, The Church of Jesus Christ of Latter-day Saints is not just another church, devoted to improving people's lives and making them happier. It is that, but it is also more. It is the kingdom of God, restored to the earth by heavenly messengers, including the Father and the Son, Moroni, John the Baptist, Elijah, Peter, James, John, and others, in fulfillment of prophecy.

What is true for the individual is also true for the Church as an institution. To the extent we behave differently from other people—either the Church as an institution or as individual members—it is because of our conviction that the prophesied Restoration has occurred. There are practical, here-and-now benefits from such practices as abstinence from alcohol and tobacco, payment of one-tenth of our income to the Church, service as missionaries, voluntary service as lay ministers, or maintenance and operation of a large welfare system. But for the real significance of these and other phenomena, one must look beyond their immediate practical consequences and see them as elements of a larger, eternal picture.

Many people, having come to an understanding of these things, have become adherents. If you are among those, I welcome you. But the purpose of this book, as I stated at the outset, is to assist not just those who want to join, but those who want to understand what we believe and why.

FOR FURTHER READING

GENERAL OVERVIEW

Ludlow, Daniel H., general editor. *Encyclopedia of Mormonism.* 5 vols. New York: Macmillan Publishing Company, 1992.

Ludlow, Victor L. *Principles and Practices of the Restored Gospel.* Salt Lake City: Deseret Book Company, 1992.

McConkie, Bruce R. *A New Witness for the Articles of Faith.* Salt Lake City: Deseret Book Company, 1985.

———. *Mormon Doctrine.* Salt Lake City: Bookcraft, 1966.

Richards, LeGrand. *A Marvelous Work and a Wonder.* Salt Lake City: Deseret Book Company, 1976.

Talmage, James E. *Articles of Faith.* Classics in Mormon Literature edition. Salt Lake City: Deseret Book Company, 1981.

———. *Jesus the Christ.* Classics in Mormon Literature edition. Salt Lake City: Deseret Book Company, 1982.

ARCHAEOLOGICAL WORKS

Allen, Joseph L. *Exploring the Lands of the Book of Mormon.* Brigham Young University Print Services, 1989.

Hansen, L. Taylor. *He Walked the Americas.* Amherst, Wisconsin: Amherst Press, 1963.

Nibley, Hugh. *An Approach to the Book of Mormon.* Third edition. Salt Lake City: Deseret Book Company, 1988.

———. *Lehi in the Desert; The World of the Jaredites; There Were Jaredites.* Salt Lake City: Deseret Book Company, 1988.

Sorenson, John L. *An Ancient American Setting for the Book of Mormon.* Salt Lake City: Deseret Book Company, 1985.

STYLISTIC WORKS

Reynolds, Noel B., editor. *Book of Mormon Authorship: New Light on Ancient Origins.* Vol. 7. Religious Studies Center. Provo, Utah: Brigham Young University, 1982.

Washburn, J. N. *The Contents, Structure and Authorship of the Book of Mormon.* Salt Lake City: Bookcraft, 1954.

Welch, John W. *Chiasmus in Antiquity.* Gerstenberg Verglag: Hildesheim, 1981.